B. Smith's

ENTERTAINING and COOKING for FRIENDS

mith's

ENTERTAINING
and COOKING for FRIENDS

BARBARA
SMITH

WITH KATHLEEN CROMWELL

PHOTOGRAPHS BY GENTL & HYERS

Artisan New York

Design: Helene Silverman

Published in 1995 by Artisan,

a division of Workman Publishing Company, Inc.

708 Broadway

New York, NY 10003

Library of Congress Cataloging-in-Publication Data

Smith, Barbara, 1949–

B. Smith's entertaining and cooking for friends / Barbara Smith,

with Kathleen Cromwell ; photographs by Gentl & Hyers

Includes index.

ISBN 1-57965-161-5

1. Entertaining.   2. Cookery.   1. Cromwell, Kathleen.   II. Title.

TX731.S487   1995

6428.4—dc20   94-45991

CIP

Printed in Japan

10 9 8 7 6 5 4 3 2

First paperback edition, 2000

for my mother,

Florence Claybrook Smith,

and

my maternal grandmother,

Hart Claybrook

Contents

INTRODUCTION   8

THE PARTIES

A Cocktail Party for Business and Pleasure   12

A Valentine's Dinner for Two   28

A Picnic at the Beach   44

A Formal Dinner for Eight   62

A Kwanzaa/Christmas Buffet   78

THE RECIPES

Appetizers   98

Soups   102

Salads   110

Pasta   120

Seafood   130

Meat and Poultry   142

Side Dishes   152

Desserts and Breads   158

ACKNOWLEDGMENTS   170

CREDITS   171

CONVERSION CHART   172

INDEX   173

INTRODUCTION

My earliest memories are ones of family gatherings, when all the relatives got together: my mom, dad, and three brothers, my grandparents, aunts, uncles, and cousins. There were so many of us that at Christmas we had to eat dinner in shifts!

It was my mother and my maternal grandmother—a large, robust, beautiful woman with the fitting name of Hart—who taught me how to cook, and I had plenty of opportunities to observe Mom, Grandma Hart, and my three aunts—Mabel, Hattie, and Nellie—cooking up a storm for church picnics and holiday meals, bake sales, Sunday dinners for visiting preachers, funerals, and weddings. All of these events required ample supplies of food, and these women always rose to the occasion with a zest and spirit that filled the house, along with the aromas of whatever they were cooking.

Everywhere one looked at home, there was food in various stages of preparation: yeast bread rising on the heating grate, freshly baked fruit pies cooling on the window sill, stews simmering on the big stove, and garden vegetables heaped on the kitchen table. And always the food was at its freshest: eggs from Grandma's chickens, newly baked bread right out of the oven, plums, peaches, apples, cherries, and pears off our trees, grapes from the arbor, and milk delivered in bottles or picked up from the local dairy.

Even my dad got in on it with his homemade wine and root beer; he served the latter, along with big bowls of buttered popcorn, on Friday nights when the boxing matches were on television. The fighting wasn't of interest to me, but the snacks sure were!

A sense of anticipation spread throughout the house whenever guests were expected. Polishing silver and waxing the furniture were two of my responsibilities, and I did them gladly for I loved it when everything shined and our warm, pleasant house was at its loveliest. This was when special things were brought out, and whether it was a pretty bowl or a fancy serving platter or an antique vase, I learned that these small touches could help transform a room.

The lessons weren't lost when I left my hometown in western Pennsylvania for a modeling career in New

York City. I never let the fact that I lived in a small apartment stop me from entertaining. Even with a limited budget—not to mention limited space—I was able to make my place look festive by, say, using candles and flowers in interesting and unexpected ways.

I don't remember my mother ever bringing fresh cut flowers into the house; it would have seemed out of place, I suppose, since we had a beautiful garden outside. It wasn't until I got to New York and became an apartment dweller, without a yard or garden to look out on, that I understood the need for flowers to bring brightness and color indoors. With the arrival of Korean grocers in New York neighborhoods, a large variety of fairly inexpensive cut flowers became available, and the farmers' markets also always have wonderful seasonal flowers.

Opposite: Saundra Parks, who often handles the flower arrangements for special events at B. Smith's restaurant, in the rooftop café. Above: *The restaurant attracts a wonderful mix of people, including actor/director Douglas Turner Ward.*

When I opened my first restaurant (B. Smith's, in New York's theater district), I wanted to make a statement with flowers. The look had to be distinctly feminine, but I wasn't interested in dainty or demure arrangements. Rather, I envisioned bold, sculptural assemblages that would add drama and elegance to the room. Saundra Parks of Daily Blossom helped me realize that vision. (Saundra also handled all the flowers for my wedding and helped me create a one-of-a-kind fantasy that Dan and I, and my stepdaughter Dana, will always remember.)

Helping to create fantasies is one of the reasons I became a fashion model; that, and the opportunity to travel. My modeling career took me all over the world, and I loved to sample the food wherever I went, experiencing a variety of new tastes and flavors from the spiciness of Caribbean cuisine to the richness of European pastries—especially those Viennese cakes!

When my modeling career was over, it seemed natural to open a restaurant that would offer the different kinds of food I loved and that would provide a gathering place for the rich variety of people I enjoyed meeting. I was still getting people together and feeding them, giving them an opportunity to meet and converse—it was just on a slightly larger scale than during my studio apartment days!

The menu at B. Smith's includes the dishes I grew up with, like smothered pork chops, pan-fried whiting, and sweet potato pecan pie. But it also reflects the influences of my travels: the profiteroles I first sampled in Vienna, the olive tapenade eaten at a café in Greece, and the pasta I fell in love with in a trattoria in Rome. (You'll find all of these recipes, which I've adapted for the home kitchen, in this book.)

But whether I am entertaining 10 people in an 800-square-foot space or a crowd of 80 in my rooftop café, my goal is always to host the kind of party I like going to. No matter where you entertain or how many guests you invite, you want to create an atmosphere that sets the right tone and mood. There are a range of entertaining possibilities, from a celebratory party where lots of activities are planned and noise is anticipated to a quiet dinner for two where candlelight plays a big role, from a casual supper with friends where the food is served family-style to a formal dinner for business colleagues where several different courses are served.

No matter what type of party you plan, the objectives remain the same: to make your guests feel welcome with warm hospitality and good food and drink, and to keep the buzz—talk, music, energy, and movement—alive.

Over the years my restaurant has attracted a wonderful mix of people—from the local regulars who hang out to the visitors who drop in—from all walks of life including the worlds of business, politics, fashion, sports, and entertainment. Celebrities like Lena Horne, Maya Angelou, Jane Alexander, Denzel Washington, Geraldo Rivera, Spike Lee, Gloria Steinem, Luther Vandross, and Douglas Turner Ward—the actor/director who founded the Negro Ensemble Company—come in, as do tourists from Topeka and the family who lives up the street. When I entertain at home, I like to invite the same sort of interesting mix of people. It's always more interesting to be creative in combining people who are in different lines of work, come from a variety of places, and have backgrounds that are dissimilar.

I wanted my restaurant to be more than just an elegant place to eat and socialize, however. I also wanted it to be a platform for the causes I was getting involved in—issues involving women, children, and minorities—so I donated space for political gatherings. The idea was to get business accomplished in as enjoyable a manner as possible, and this formula has been very successful. Chapter 2, "A Cocktail Party for Business and Pleasure," suggests a variety of ways in which you can entertain work associates in a personalized manner.

The ideas, recipes, and menus in this book are simply suggestions that you can use as a springboard for your own entertainment needs and party plans. I discuss the ways I have entertained on different occasions—an intimate Valentine's Day dinner, a cocktail gathering for business associates, a holiday buffet for family and friends, a formal dinner for eight, a beach picnic and a party for children—not so you can duplicate these scenarios necessarily, but so you can use these examples as a spark to ignite ideas for your own events.

This isn't so much a "how-to" book as it is a "why not?" one. Why not dress formally for a special dinner at home? Why not have an elegant outdoor party on the beach? Why not invite the family over even though you don't have enough chairs? Why not let the kids have a party of their own while you're preparing dinner for the adults? Use this book as a catalyst, not a crutch, to help get you over the hurdle of entertainment timidity. If you're new at this, start small—invite just one or two people over for dinner. Make it easy on yourself by having a dinner party with family and close friends before you work up to entertaining business associates.

Fear of failure will only limit you, so don't be afraid to take risks. Mistakes are part of the fun. I personally would never try out a new recipe on guests (though I know people who have done so with great success), but I wouldn't think twice about making some dramatic gesture like stacking up a pyramid of glasses and making a Champagne fountain. There are far worse things than broken glasses and spilled Champagne. This attitude will help you maintain a sense of spontaneity, which is essential no matter what the occasion may be. An event should flow, not feel "planned," no matter how much planning went into it! If you're prepared to improvise (spread the picnic blankets on the living room floor if it rains), you can enjoy being creative all the more.

Finally, remember that it's not just the guests who should be enjoying themselves; you should be having a good time, too. If you relax and have fun, so will everyone else.

Entertaining is all about taking risks and having fun. This Champagne fountain captures the sense of drama and spontaneity that can make a party memorable.

a cocktail party for business and pleasure

WHEN I PLAN what I like to call a cocktail gathering, that's exactly what I do: I gather together a mix of people in the hopes that good conversations will start up, interesting connections will be made, and new friendships will be forged.

The purpose of a gathering like this is to meet, greet, eat, and drink within a specific time frame—usually a couple of hours in the early evening. It's a transitional period between work and dinner that allows people to engage in casual chat or business networking while enjoying a couple of drinks and a little light food.

The starting time depends on your schedule. On leisurely weekends things can begin fairly early. During the summer months, we sometimes have

a cocktail party 13

people over for drinks around five. If I plan something during the week, though, I keep in mind that most people are coming from work so I start a little later—around six or seven o'clock. Don't start any later than that unless you plan to offer dinner as well.

The length of the party depends on its purpose and is entirely up to you. I am involved in a great many political fund-raisers, and I've found that a cocktail gathering is a perfect way to mix business and pleasure—after all, the more relaxed people are, the more generous they are likely to be! In those cases I've found that three hours is necessary to give everyone a chance to socialize and also to allow time for brief speeches, discussions, presentations, and so on. When the event goes on that long,

Preceding page: *Actor John Terrell*. Above: *Guests Dennis Franklin and Karen Wadkins.* Right: *Guests of honor Marilyn and Alan Nicholson, with my husband, Dan, enjoying the host's art collection.*

though, I always end by serving coffee and some little sweets. If it's strictly a social affair, however, two hours is generally sufficient.

When thinking about the location for the party, keep in mind that you don't have to limit yourself to your home or apartment. A whole range of options is available, so expand your horizons and get out of the house! In the summer, invite your guests to gather outdoors and socialize in the sunlight and fresh air—a nice alternative to the dimly lit, smoky gatherings that are still popular. A garden or patio is a good place for an alfresco affair, and if you have neither of these, check out a local botanical garden.

Libraries, boats, and zoos are fun settings, and for a dramatic event consider your local theater, which may be willing to rent out the space on evenings when there are no performances. Bear in mind that if you rent a space, you may have to make arrangements several weeks or even months in advance.

The location you choose will help establish the mood you're trying to set. My gathering, which was held for Marilyn and Alan Nicholson— out-of-town friends of Dan's whom I hadn't spent much time with and wanted to get to know better—took place at the apartment/gallery of art dealer friends whose collection is displayed throughout the rooms. It's an interesting and sophisticated setting where the visual benefits of a gallery are combined with the comforts of a private home.

Dan and I wanted our guests to experience this unique space and to see a bit of what makes New York

THE INVITATION: A SOCIAL CONTRACT

An invitation is the first step in what is essentially a social contract between host and guest. The responsibility of the inviter is to supply as much information as possible about the event; the more knowledge your guests have, the more comfortable they will be about accepting your invitation.

Of course you have to provide the date, time, location, and purpose of the event, but you should also include anything else you think your guests might need to know in advance. For example, I make it a point to mention the appropriate attire, because nothing makes a person feel more awkward than showing up in jeans when everyone else is in formal wear. Or if it's a swimming party, I remind my guests to bring swimsuits. Also, it's often helpful to enclose a little map or drawing with directions to the party site.

The invitee is obliged to heed the information given and, if he or she accepts the invitation, to comply with any request such as to B.Y.O.B. or to come in a costume. And all invitees, whether they will be attending or not, should always R.S.V.P. well before the event so the host can plan accordingly.

A general rule of thumb is to send out invitations two to three weeks in advance—unless it's a big affair and/or is taking place during a busy social season, in which case you should send them out six weeks in advance. For more casual get-togethers with close friends you can sometimes get away with only a week's notice.

Whether you mail, phone, or fax your invitations, if you haven't gotten a response, it's always a good idea to give a follow-up call a week or so before the event. You never know if mail went undelivered, messages got erased, or faxes were lost. Then again, someone may have simply forgotten to respond.

City so special. The art on the walls provided a fabulous backdrop for the get-together, and small groupings of couches and chairs created spots where people could sit and talk.

We assembled an assortment of friends whom we thought Marilyn (an advertising executive) and Alan (a real-estate developer) would find fun and interesting. They represented a range of urban pursuits: a vice-president at the television production company where Dan works, a friend with whom I used to model, an actor, a TV producer, a lawyer in the fashion business, the owner of a salon, and of course our art dealer friends.

Part of the fun of a party of this type is introducing people to one another and mentioning something specific that will provoke their interest or curiosity: "I'd like you to meet Dennis, who was a quarterback when he was at U. of M. Dennis, John played a football player in his most recent film role." I'm particularly pleased when I can bring together two people who can be helpful to one another—for example, introducing a music video producer who is looking for a location to a real-estate broker who specializes in commercial properties.

Gradually the party reaches its crescendo, when the initial shy introductions and preliminary chitchat are over, people are more at ease, and the talk is more animated. You can hear a number of intriguing conversations going on simultaneously and everyone seems to be pleasantly engaged. It's especially gratifying

when colleagues and business associates are brought together with friends. I like to combine my professional and personal lives in this way and to bring together individuals who might otherwise never meet.

If you are giving your party in a place other than your own home, you will need to arrange for certain supplies to be brought in. For my cocktail party I had the ice, liquor, and glassware (which I was renting) delivered to the site. I provided the flowers, napkins, and serving platters, and I made my own food; Reese and Bill Karg, the owners of the gallery, furnished plates and bowls.

Above: *Anderson Phillips, owner of Scissors Beauty Salon in New York, came to the party dressed in a piece that looked like African art, and was in fact purchased on one of his trips to Africa.* Opposite: *TV producer Gene Davis.*

The way you choose to invite your guests will be determined primarily by the number you are inviting. My gathering was a very impromptu affair for twelve, so I phoned or faxed people to invite them. If you plan on having more than twenty and/or you have a more formal event in mind, written invitations would be a better choice.

You can keep things simple when you decorate your space. I did a minimal amount of work in preparing for this soirée because the surrounding art was a major part of the ambience. I simply added a few personal touches such as arrangements of fresh flowers, some handsomely designed paper napkins, a few pretty serving platters, and monogrammed hand towels for the bathroom.

There are all kinds of ways to get a space that is not yours to reflect your own style. Colorful balloon bouquets for a celebration, like a birthday or a bon voyage party, create a bright note. For a dramatic effect try using an assortment of candles in artful arrangements. You can even rent plants to bring a little greenery into the background.

When planning your menu for a cocktail event, you have to decide not only what to serve but how it will be served. Will it be displayed buffet-style or passed around on a tray? I set out my cocktail hors d'oeuvres in strategic places to ensure that everyone didn't congregate in one spot. Instead they could circulate around the room and mingle with one another while sampling the food at the various locations.

When you have a lot of people, it's nice to have some food set out and some served by a helper. There are a number of advantages to food being passed around. For one thing it is an elegant way for the food to be presented—held aloft on a tray and then proffered to an individual guest. It also allows you to serve things piping hot—the food can go straight from the oven onto the tray and be delivered to your guests in minutes.

The menu for my party consisted of easy-to-eat finger foods served at room temperature. I provided sauces on the side, so that my guests had the option to dip or not depending on whether they wanted to avoid extra calories or possibly messy drips.

When I planned my menu I wanted to include basic dishes like the chicken on skewers, heartier fare like the baby lamb chops, and interesting touches like the leek and potato pancakes with smoked salmon. A number of the dishes I selected can be made in advance: The lamb chops, shrimp, chicken, and even the potato pancakes can be prepared ahead of time and reheated; even the fruit—served on skewers—can be cut up ahead of time.

Deciding on the quantity of food is simple mathematics. If you are serving cocktails right before seating people for dinner, figure four

arrived at 96. There were six different dishes I wanted to serve, so I made, on average, 16 of each hors d'oeuvre. (I also mixed up two cups of Vineyard Lobster Dip and served it in a hollowed-out head of red cabbage, surrounded by chips, raw vegetables and toasted pita triangles.)

Some hors d'oeuvres I made more or less of, depending on the ingredients. For instance, I had 20 skewers of chicken, figuring almost everyone would eat a couple of these hearty offerings. On the other hand I served only 12 portions of mixed fruit on skewers; the fruit was more of a palate cleanser and one for each guest was sufficient. I had 16 each of the mini crab cakes, the petite potato leek pancakes, and the marinated baby lamb chops, and 18 of the skewered shrimp with plantains.

While deciding how much food to provide, take into consideration how much you will be able to prepare. You may want to make only a portion and have the rest catered—perhaps providing the caterers with your own recipes. And a good general rule is: The more people, the simpler the food. After all, when you have a lot of guests to entertain you don't want to be preoccupied with the food, so the less complicated the better. Your menu should strike a balance between sweet and savory, smooth and crunchy, and raw and cooked ingredients, so that your guests can experience a wide range of textures and tastes.

As for beverages, if possible find out the preferences of your guests beforehand and stock their favorite drinks. In general, though, when I want to keep things simple, I have just white and red wine and vodka and mixers. If your party calls for greater variety, you can provide a more extensive bar with a full array of liquors and mixers, plus wine, beer, and Champagne. I always have plenty of sparkling and mineral waters on hand, along with fruit and vegetable juices and nonalcoholic beer. You can generally figure on two to three drinks per person in the course of a couple of hours.

A cocktail gathering is an excellent way of bringing together informally a variety of people, whether for business or pleasure. Relatively little last minute cooking and precision timing is required, as most of the food preparation can be completed in advance. And, it provides you with an opportunity to show off your skills as a mixologist! Experiment with new drinks like the one that follows.

TRIBECA COCKTAIL

3 ounces Champagne
3 ounces cranberry juice
1 ounce Absolut Citron
Splash of Chambord (optional)
Lemon wedge, for garnish

Place ice in a large red wine glass; pour in a shot of the vodka; slowly pour in Champagne until half the glass is filled; top off with cranberry juice and a splash of Chambord, if desired; garnish with a wedge of fresh lemon.

Makes 1 drink

to six hors d'oeuvres per person. Otherwise plan on providing a bit more—closer to six to eight hors d'oeuvres for each guest. Multiply the number of guests by the number of hors d'oeuvres, and then you can decide how many different types of food you will provide.

For example, for my party I figured on six to eight hors d'oeuvres per person. (It is always better to err on the high side. Leftovers are easier to deal with than running out of food mid-party.) Choosing the higher number (eight), I multiplied it by the number of guests and

STOCKING THE BAR

Here are some components of a well-stocked bar, which you can adjust according to your own and your guests' preferences.

At the very least have these basics on hand. Start with one bottle of each and add more if the event requires. (I always like to keep an extra bottle of vodka in the freezer because of its everlasting popularity.)

Vodka
Gin
Scotch
Tequila
Rum (light and dark)
Bourbon

Supply plenty of mixers, which help to stretch the liquor.

Sparkling water
Club soda
Cola
Diet cola
Ginger ale
Tonic water
Orange juice
Grapefruit juice
Cranberry juice
Tomato juice
Pineapple juice

There aren't any steadfast rules today about wine and food. You may want to put on a wine tasting with your friends in order to find some selections you especially like. Have a selection of wine and beer on hand.

WHITE WINE
Chardonnay
Pinot Grigio
Blanc de Blanc

RED WINE
Cabernet Sauvignon
Merlot
Pinot Noir

SPARKLERS
Champagne
Sparkling cider
Sparkling wine

BEER
Light
Dark

Keep some Cognac in the house for after dinner, and stock your bar with some sweet liqueurs (which you can also cook with or pour over ice cream for an easy dessert).

Grand Marnier
Amaretto

Kahlúa
Crème de cacao
Cream sherry
Cointreau
Benedictine
Sweet vermouth

And of course all the items you need to make the drinks!

Oranges
Lemons
Limes
Maraschino cherries
Olives
Bitters
Tabasco sauce
Worcestershire sauce
Blender
Ice bucket
Tongs
Corkscrew
Champagne stopper
Can opener
Jigger measure
Cocktail shaker
Pitcher and bar spoon
Zester
Strainer
Bottle cap remover

Three things you need an almost endless supply of:

Glasses (highball, wine, and Champagne)
Ice
Cocktail napkins

Restaurant supply stores have large selections of sturdy, inexpensive glasses that can be bought in bulk. I prefer an all-purpose glass, like a large red wine glass, that can also be used to serve beer, mineral water, and mixed drinks—functional yet elegant. No matter what kind of glasses you use, have plenty of them on hand for those people who have a tendency to set their drink down and forget where they've put it!

Some yields to keep in mind:

1 bottle of Champagne
= 4 to 6 flute glasses

1 bottle of wine
= 4 to 6 glasses

1½-liter bottle of wine
= 8 to 12 glasses

1 case/12 bottles of wine
= 72 drinks

MENU

Shrimp and Plantains on Skewers with Mango Mayonnaise

Potato Leek Pancakes with Smoked Salmon,
Crème Fraîche, and Caviar

Gingery Chicken Kabobs with Honey Mustard Sauce

Pan-Fried Crab Cakes with Chili Mayonnaise

Vineyard Lobster Dip with Chips, Raw Vegetables, and Toasted Pita

Marinated Party Lamb Chops with Mint Dip

Fresh Fruit on Skewers with Crème Anglaise

Tribeca Cocktail

Red and White Wine

Vodka and Mixers

Beer

Mineral Water

SHRIMP AND PLANTAINS ON SKEWERS WITH MANGO MAYONNAISE

I adapted this recipe from my Grilled Scampi with Mango Glacé, a main-course dish. The sauce here is a bit thicker, which makes it easier to handle as a party food.

2   POUNDS MEDIUM-SIZE SHRIMP (ABOUT 36),
      PEELED AND DEVEINED
1   RECIPE MARINADE FROM GRILLED SHRIMP
      WITH MANGO GLACÉ AND PLANTAINS
      (SEE PAGE 133)
    VEGETABLE OIL
3   LARGE PLANTAINS, PEELED, EACH CUT INTO
      12 SLICES
    MANGO MAYONNAISE (RECIPE FOLLOWS)

Place the shrimp in a shallow dish or plastic container, and pour the marinade over them. Cover and marinate for 4 to 6 hours in the refrigerator.

Preheat the broiler.

Transfer the shrimp to a broiling pan, and broil for 2 to 3 minutes on each side, until just cooked. Set aside to cool.

Heat just enough oil to cover the bottom of a large skillet, and cook the plantain slices for 1 minute on each side or until golden and tender. Set them aside on a plate to cool.

Thread 2 shrimp and 2 plantain slices onto each small skewer, and serve with Mango Mayonnaise as a dipping sauce.

Makes 18 skewers

MANGO MAYONNAISE
1   CUP MAYONNAISE
½   CUP MANGO PURÉE (FRESH OR FROZEN,
      THAWED)
¼   CUP SOUR CREAM
2   TABLESPOONS FRESH LIME JUICE
¼   TEASPOON SALT
¼   TEASPOON GROUND BLACK PEPPER

Stir together all the ingredients in a medium-size bowl. Cover and chill until needed.

Makes about 1½ cups

2 POUNDS BONELESS, SKINLESS CHICKEN BREASTS

MARINADE

2	TABLESPOONS PEANUT OIL
2	TABLESPOONS OYSTER SAUCE
1	TABLESPOON GRATED FRESH GINGER
1	TEASPOON MINCED GARLIC
¼	TEASPOON TABASCO SAUCE
¼	TEASPOON SALT
¼	TEASPOON GROUND BLACK PEPPER

SAUCE

¼	CUP HONEY
¼	CUP DIJON MUSTARD
2	TABLESPOONS FRESH LEMON JUICE

Soak 20 six-inch bamboo skewers in water for 15 minutes.

Cut the chicken into ¹/₂-inch-wide strips and thread them onto skewers. Arrange the skewers in a single layer in a shallow dish or plastic container. Mix the marinade ingredients together in a small bowl, and pour this over the chicken. Cover, and marinate for 4 to 6 hours in the refrigerator.

Preheat the oven to 350° F.

Remove the skewers from the marinade and lay them out on baking sheets. Bake for 12 to 15 minutes, or just until the chicken is tender.

The kabobs can also be deep fried. Heat the oil to 350° F in a deep skillet or electric fryer and cook the skewers, a few at a time, for 3 to 4 minutes, or until golden brown.

Meanwhile, mix the honey, mustard, and lemon juice together in a small bowl. Serve the chicken skewers, with the sauce alongside for dipping.

Makes 20 kabobs

GINGERY CHICKEN KABOBS WITH HONEY MUSTARD SAUCE

These kabobs can be prepared in advance and then bathed in the marinade until party time. It takes only minutes for them to cook, and they are easy to handle with or without the sauce. I've found them to be a big hit at parties for kids.

Pan-Fried Crab Cakes with Chili Mayonnaise

These scrumptious crab cakes are always in demand at the restaurant and seem to impress guests whenever I serve them at home. A petite version is an ideal finger food that can be dipped into the spicy Chili Mayonnaise.

- 1   TABLESPOON UNSALTED BUTTER
- ½   CUP FINELY CHOPPED ONION
- ½   CUP FINELY CHOPPED CELERY
- 1   POUND FRESH CRABMEAT
- ¾   CUP UNSEASONED DRIED BREAD CRUMBS
- 1   LARGE EGG
- 1   TABLESPOON MAYONNAISE
- 1   TABLESPOON SOUR CREAM
- 1   TEASPOON CHOPPED FRESH DILL
- 1   TEASPOON OLD BAY SEASONING
- ½   TEASPOON GARLIC POWDER
- 2   TABLESPOONS VEGETABLE OIL
-     CHILI MAYONNAISE (RECIPE FOLLOWS)

Heat the butter in a small skillet, and sauté the onions and celery until softened. Set aside.

In a large mixing bowl, stir together the crabmeat, ¼ cup of the bread crumbs, the onions and celery, and the egg, mayonnaise, sour cream, dill, Old Bay Seasoning, and garlic powder. Mix thoroughly. Mold the mixture into 1-inch patties, and coat them with the remaining bread crumbs.

Heat the oil in a large skillet and cook the crab cakes on both sides for 4 to 6 minutes, until lightly golden brown. Serve immediately, with Chili Mayonnaise alongside.

Makes sixteen 1-inch or four 4-inch crab cakes

CHILI MAYONNAISE

- 1   CUP MAYONNAISE
- 2   TABLESPOONS FINELY CHOPPED FRESH JALAPEÑO PEPPER
-     FEW DROPS OF TABASCO SAUCE

Mix all the ingredients together in a small bowl. Cover and chill until needed.

Makes 1 cup

Potato Leek Pancakes

These versatile pancakes take on many attitudes and adapt to any occasion. For an elegant affair serve them as a first course warm, over mixed salad greens, with smoked salmon, crème fraîche, and caviar. Served mini-size, they make perfect cocktail hors d'oeuvres.

2 CUPS GRATED PEELED POTATOES
1½ CUPS FINELY CHOPPED LEEKS, WHITE PART ONLY
2 LARGE EGGS, BEATEN
¼ CUP ALL-PURPOSE FLOUR
1 TEASPOON SALT
¼ TEASPOON GROUND BLACK PEPPER
VEGETABLE OIL

SALAD GREENS, FOR SERVING
SMOKED SALMON, CRÈME FRAÎCHE AND CAVIAR, OR CHUNKY APPLESAUCE, FOR GARNISH

Mix the potatoes, leeks, eggs, flour, salt, and pepper together in a large bowl until thoroughly combined. Heat just enough oil to cover the bottom of a medium-size skillet. Spoon one-eighth of the mixture into the center of the skillet and spread it out slightly to form a 3-inch circle. Cook over medium heat until golden on the underside. Using a large metal spatula, turn it over and cook until golden on the other side and cooked through. Repeat with the remaining mixture, keeping the cooked pancakes warm in the oven.

Serve warm with smoked salmon, crème fraîche and caviar, or with chunky applesauce.

Makes eight 3-inch or four 6-inch pancakes

VINEYARD LOBSTER DIP

I have friends who can't wait to go on their annual summer vacation in New England in order to taste their first lobster roll of the season. Several places on Martha's Vineyard, for instance, serve up exquisite lobster sandwiches—the inspiration for this fabulous dip.

2   CUPS FINELY CHOPPED COOKED LOBSTER
1   CUP FINELY CHOPPED CELERY
½   CUP FINELY CHOPPED RED ONION
1   CUP MAYONNAISE
3   TABLESPOONS FRESH LEMON JUICE
¼   TEASPOON SALT
¼   TEASPOON GROUND WHITE PEPPER
     CHOPPED FRESH PARSLEY, FOR GARNISH

Stir all the ingredients together in a large bowl until well combined. Garnish with the parsley, and serve immediately as a dip for assorted crackers, pita bread triangles, and raw vegetables.

Makes 4 cups

Variation: To serve this as an appetizer, spoon the mixture into avocado halves and sprinkle with fresh parsley.

Marinated Party Lamb Chops with Mint Dip

These tasty chops are extremely easy to prepare, the major effort involved being to turn them frequently as they soak in the marinade.

16   SMALL RIB LAMB CHOPS
     (ABOUT 2 OUNCES EACH)

MARINADE

½   CUP OLIVE OIL
¼   CUP FRESH LEMON JUICE
½   TEASPOON SALT
½   TEASPOON COARSELY GROUND BLACK PEPPER
2   CLOVES GARLIC, MINCED
1   BAY LEAF
2   SPRIGS FRESH ROSEMARY, CHOPPED
1   SPRIG FRESH PARSLEY, CHOPPED

Place the lamb chops in a shallow dish. Combine the marinade ingredients in a small bowl and pour over the lamb chops. Cover and refrigerate for at least 3 hours, turning frequently.

Broil, grill, or sauté the lamb for 3 to 4 minutes on each side according to taste. Serve the lamb chops warm or hot on a large platter with Mint Dip in a vegetable container alongside.

Makes 8 servings

MINT DIP

⅓   CUP CHOPPED FRESH MINT LEAVES
⅔   CUP CIDER VINEGAR
⅔   CUP SUGAR
⅔   CUP WATER
2   TABLESPOONS CORNSTARCH

Combine the mint leaves, vinegar, sugar, and water in a small saucepan. Bring to a boil, then cook over medium heat until reduced to about ⅔ cup. Mix the cornstarch with a little cold water until smooth. Gradually stir the cornstarch mixture into the hot liquid until blended. Bring to a boil and cook 1 minute. Cool and serve in a hollowed out vegetable, such as a winter squash, green or red bell pepper half, or a small eggplant.

Makes about ⅔ cup

a valentine's dinner for two

VALENTINE'S DAY is my favorite holiday

because it's the ultimate day to celebrate love and romance. A beautiful way of expressing how you feel about your beloved—spouse, lover, son, daughter, or "significant other"—is by making a great meal for just the two of you. With a small amount of effort you can easily transform a dinner at home into a very special evening.

Romance frequently gets forgotten in our busy lives. We make business dates for lunch all the time, but when was the last time you surprised your significant other with an invitation to a rendezvous in your own living room? Of course you don't have to wait until February 14. Choose a particular time you want to set aside, and share an intimate, elegant dinner.

You might want to celebrate New Year's Eve this way, for example, as a cozy alternative to the usual crowded frenzy of restaurants that night.

Dan and I eat many meals at our restaurants, so it's a treat when we can have a quiet dinner at home. On Valentine's Day we like to stay in and have a private party for two: eat a fabulous meal, drink good Champagne, share corny toasts, and dance to our favorite music.

A celebration like this can be very special when your everyday surroundings are transformed into a private retreat. Rearrange the furniture to create an ambience of coziness and comfort.

This is not the time to eat at the formal dining table. For these dinners with Dan I usually use a small round table so we can sit close together and hold hands during the meal. I move the plant that normally resides there and place the table under a favorite painting of ours. The idea is to change things around so that, for this one night, your surroundings are altered and your everyday space becomes a transformative place.

Often the most comfortable setting for an intimate dinner à deux *is your own home. Candles, roses, Champagne, and a special menu helped create the mood for the Valentine's dinner I planned for my husband, Dan.*

Elements of romantic style: elegant china, sterling silver, and a perfect red rose.

yourself to just a single centerpiece. I like to put a number of small arrangements in various spots, adding splashes of color throughout the apartment and making the whole place smell scrumptious!

As for the ambient sound, make sure your favorite music is on hand to create the right mood. On our first Valentine's Day, I gave Dan an Aaron Neville tape as a gift, so of course he played it at our little dinner party.

Surprise that special someone with a different kind of invitation: a single rose in a vase with a note attached, or a handwritten message on scented stationery secretly slipped into a pocket, a briefcase, or a purse.

If there's a color that is meaningful to your relationship, have a dash of it somewhere on the invitation. Red is our color because it's symbolic of strawberries, which were in season when Dan and I first met.

The dress is definitely formal. How often do you get to wear those gowns and tuxedos that conjure romance? Though elegant and exquisite, evening wear can also make one long to remove the layers of formality, which adds a nice edge to an occasion like this. Keep in mind, though, that you may be spending some time in the kitchen, so it's best to avoid dresses with long, loose sleeves or complicated jewelry that could get in the way of your cooking duties.

For this special occasion I planned a meal to include our favorite dishes, because this dinner *à deux* should have all the foods you both like.

It was Dan who pointed out what each of the items on the menu sym-

For the same reason, you don't want to use the day-to-day tablewear. Instead, bring out all of your good things and plan on spending as much time dressing the table as you do yourself. Cover the table with your finest cloth, put out your best dishes, and dig out the set of silver. I always use my red linen napkins.

To set the atmosphere, I replace the regular light bulbs with pink ones to create a rosy glow, and I also place candles around the room. Fresh flowers can be a bright, fragrant addition to the room or table. Don't limit

bolized: the roasted tomato soup is a reflection of our hearts; the lamb, like love, is tender (as well as one of our favorite dishes); and the mocha torte is, simply, the perfect dessert.

To get off to a festive start, Dan and I opened a bottle of La Grande Dame Champagne that we had received as a wedding present and had saved for just such an occasion, and raised our crystal glasses in toasts to one another. As we nibbled on Beluga caviar spread on toast points we sipped our Champagne, which, in fact, we drank throughout the meal.

Only food that can be made in advance belongs on this menu, to ensure that practically no time is spent in the kitchen during the evening. You may want to plan on a menu that allows for between-course activities, like dancing.

The soup I selected is not only delicious and a gorgeous red that fits right into my color scheme, but it can also be prepared beforehand and reheated. The baby lamb chops—tender, moist, and redolent of fresh rosemary—are sautéed just until pink and medium-rare. The Madeira sauce is a simple reduction of the meat drippings and takes only a few minutes to create since the wine cooks off quickly. You can either make the entrée on the spot (wear a gorgeous apron over your evening gown!) or prepare the lamb shortly beforehand and keep it warm in the oven. Prepare the potatoes au gratin in advance and keep them covered on top of the stove; reheat them just before serving. The mocha torte with crème anglaise and rasp-berry coulis—a chocolaty sweet finish to our special dinner—was made the day before so it could set and chill.

An equally elegant and delicious menu that I've served to Dan on Valentine's Day includes Shrimp Chardonnay Soup, Linguine with Roasted Plum Tomato Sauce, and strawberries dipped in chocolate. The soup is a lovely blush color, and the linguine is a beautiful tumble of pasta and rich red tomatoes. The combination of ripe strawberries and chocolate always looks great (and they are easy to prepare and can be made in advance). Use the largest, most succulent strawberries you can find; leave the stems intact. To prepare a chocolate dipping sauce, simply melt 6 ounces of your favorite semisweet chocolate chips with $1^1/2$ teaspoons vegetable shortening in the top of a double boiler over simmering water. Remove the melted chocolate from the heat and dip the strawberries in the warm chocolate. Place the strawberries on a foil-lined tray in the refrigerator until chocolate sets, about 20 minutes.

Instead of Champagne, you might choose a sparkling wine or a full-bodied Chardonnay. Later, serve an after-dinner liqueur, such as Grand Marnier, for a gracious end to the meal.

A definite advantage to entertaining at home is not having to worry about driving. So have that extra glass of wine if you'd like! After this meal the only transportation you will have to deal with will be waltzing yourselves into the next room.

VALENTINE'S DINNER FOR KIDS

If your significant other is a child, it can be fun to decorate the table in a way he or she will enjoy and can participate in. The two of you can make place mats out of Valentines the child received at school or ones made at home. Arrange them artfully and glue them onto a sturdy piece of cardboard. You can even get them laminated—many photo and copy shops have lamination services.

You can also make place cards using photographs of yourselves. Take pictures with a Polaroid camera, cut heart-shaped frames out of paper, and glue them to cardboard stands.

Instead of place mats, you could cover the table with a sheet of white drawing paper and set out a glass full of crayons. Let the child decorate the paper with drawings of cherubs, hearts and arrows, or whatever else might strike your Valentine's fancy!

MENU 1

Beluga Caviar on Toast Points

Roasted Plum Tomato Soup with Chèvre Croutons

Baby Lamb Chops with Madeira Sauce

Potatoes au Gratin

Mocha Torte with Crème Anglaise and Raspberry Coulis

La Grande Dame Champagne

MENU 2

Shrimp Chardonnay Soup

Tomato, Watercress, and Endive Salad with Raspberry Vinaigrette

Linguine with Roasted Plum Tomato Sauce

Strawberries Dipped in Chocolate

Chardonnay

Chianti

BABY LAMB CHOPS WITH MADEIRA SAUCE

Lamb appeared only occasionally on the dinner table when I was growing up, always in the form of a roast and always served with mint jelly. The succulence of these baby lamb chops is complemented nicely by the rosemary-flavored Madeira sauce.

½   CUP ALL-PURPOSE FLOUR

½   TEASPOON SALT

¼   TEASPOON GROUND BLACK PEPPER

16   RIB LAMB CHOPS

2   TABLESPOONS OLIVE OIL

½   CUP MADEIRA WINE

½   CUP HOMEMADE BEEF STOCK OR CANNED BROTH

¼   TEASPOON CHOPPED FRESH ROSEMARY,
     OR ⅛ TEASPOON DRIED

Stir the flour, salt, and pepper together in a small cup and spread the mixture out on a large plate. Dip the lamb chops in the flour mixture on both sides. Shake off any excess.

Heat the oil in a large skillet and sauté the chops over medium-high heat according to taste. Transfer them to a serving platter and keep warm. Pour the Madeira, stock, and rosemary into the skillet and bring to a boil, scraping up all the cooked juices from the bottom. Remove the skillet from the heat, pour the sauce over the lamb chops, and serve immediately.

Serves 4

Roasted Plum Tomato Soup with Chèvre Croutons

This soup is a beautiful velvety red that provides a colorful addition to your table. Fresh basil complements the tomato wonderfully, and because plum tomatoes are always readily available, you can make this year-round.

2	TABLESPOONS OLIVE OIL
½	CUP FINELY DICED ONION
½	CUP FINELY DICED TURNIP
½	CUP FINELY DICED CARROT
2	TEASPOONS MINCED GARLIC
4	CUPS HOMEMADE VEGETABLE OR CHICKEN STOCK, OR CANNED BROTH
¼	CUP TOMATO PASTE
3	CUPS ROASTED PLUM TOMATOES (RECIPE FOLLOWS) WITH THEIR COOKING JUICES
¼	CUP FIRMLY PACKED FRESH BASIL LEAVES
¼	CUP CHOPPED FRESH PARSLEY
3	TABLESPOONS MASCARPONE CHEESE
3	TABLESPOONS CHÈVRE
12	SMALL SLICES FRENCH BREAD
	FRESH PARSLEY LEAVES, FOR GARNISH

Heat the oil in a large saucepan over a medium-high heat, and sauté the onion, turnip, carrot, and garlic until softened. Stir in the stock, tomato paste, and roasted tomatoes together with any cooking juices. Cover and bring to a boil. Reduce the heat and simmer for 30 minutes.

Meanwhile, finely chop 1 tablespoon of the basil leaves. In a small bowl, combine the chopped basil and 1 tablespoon of the parsley with the mascarpone and chèvre. Blend thoroughly. Preheat the broiler and grill the slices of French bread until light golden brown. Spread the cheese mixture over the toasted bread.

Coarsely chop the remaining basil leaves, and stir the basil and the remaining parsley into the soup. Divide the soup among six soup bowls, and top each with two cheese croutons. Garnish with extra parsley leaves, if desired.

Makes about 7 cups (6 servings)

ROASTED PLUM TOMATOES

24	LARGE RIPE PLUM TOMATOES
2	TABLESPOONS OLIVE OIL
1	TABLESPOON CHOPPED FRESH BASIL
1	TEASPOON CHOPPED FRESH OREGANO

Preheat the oven to 325° F.

Cut the tomatoes in half crosswise, and place them in a large roasting pan. Drizzle the olive oil over them, and sprinkle the chopped herbs over the top. Roast for 45 minutes.

Let the tomatoes cool slightly. Then remove the skins and cores, and coarsely chop the flesh.

Makes about 3 cups

POTATOES AU GRATIN

This is one of the first dishes I made in Home Economics class, but it wasn't until after I graduated that I learned about adding Parmesan and Gruyère for a more sophisticated version.

⅓ CUP UNSALTED BUTTER, SOFTENED

1½ POUNDS IDAHO POTATOES, PEELED AND CUT INTO ¼-INCH-THICK SLICES

½ CUP GRATED GRUYÈRE CHEESE

½ CUP FRESHLY GRATED PARMESAN CHEESE

1 CUP HEAVY CREAM

1 TEASPOON SALT

½ TEASPOON GROUND BLACK PEPPER

⅛ TEASPOON PAPRIKA

Preheat the oven to 350° F. Butter a 1½-quart baking dish with about 1 tablespoon of the softened butter.

Arrange a layer of potatoes in the baking dish, and sprinkle some of the cheeses over them. Continue layering potatoes and cheeses until you've used them all, ending with a layer of potatoes.

In a small bowl, whisk the cream with the salt and pepper; pour this over the potatoes. Dot the remaining butter over the top, and sprinkle with the paprika. Bake for 1 to 1¼ hours, or until the potatoes are tender and golden brown on top. Let stand for 5 minutes before serving.

Serves 4

SHRIMP CHARDONNAY SOUP

A variation on Cajun drunken shrimp, which uses beer, this soup makes it abundantly clear that shrimp also love to bathe in Chardonnay! It can be a great start to a meal or a main course. Either way, you'll want some crusty bread to soak up the last of the broth.

2 TABLESPOONS UNSALTED BUTTER

½ CUP FINELY CHOPPED ONION

1 TEASPOON MINCED GARLIC

16 MEDIUM TO LARGE SHRIMP, PEELED AND DEVEINED, TAILS LEFT ON

1 CUP BOTTLED CLAM JUICE

1 CUP CHARDONNAY WINE

1 CUP TOMATO SAUCE

1 TABLESPOON CHOPPED FRESH BASIL

1 TEASPOON CHOPPED FRESH PARSLEY

½ TEASPOON SALT

¼ TEASPOON GROUND BLACK PEPPER

Melt the butter over medium heat in a large saucepan, and sauté the onion and garlic until softened. Add the shrimp and sauté for 2 to 3 minutes, just until they turn pink.

Add the clam juice, Chardonnay, and tomato sauce. Bring to a gentle boil and cook for 1 minute. Using a slotted spoon, transfer the shrimp to a serving bowl; keep warm. Raise the heat under the saucepan and reduce the broth by approximately ¼ cup. Stir in the basil, parsley, salt, and pepper. Pour the sauce over the shrimp, and serve immediately.

Makes about 4½ cups (Serves 4)

Tomato, Watercress, and Endive Salad

Watercress is readily available year-round and is a perfect way to sharpen up a salad. As part of a big meal, this dish can serve as a refreshing between-course palate cleanser.

1 LARGE HEAD BELGIAN ENDIVE,
    LEAVES SEPARATED
2 CUPS WATERCRESS SPRIGS (LARGE STEMS
    REMOVED)
4 MEDIUM-SIZE RIPE TOMATOES, CUT INTO
    WEDGES
    RASPBERRY VINAIGRETTE (RECIPE FOLLOWS)

Arrange the endive leaves on a large platter, fanning them out from the center. Roughly chop the watercress, and sprinkle it over the endive. Top with the tomato wedges, and drizzle with Raspberry Vinaigrette to taste. Serve immediately.

Serves 4

RASPBERRY VINAIGRETTE

¼ CUP SEEDLESS RASPBERRY JAM OR
    RASPBERRY COULIS (SEE PAGE 164)
¾ CUP EXTRA-VIRGIN OLIVE OIL
¼ CUP RASPBERRY VINEGAR
½ TEASPOON MINCED GARLIC
    SALT AND PEPPER TO TASTE

Whisk all the ingredients together in a small bowl. Cover and chill until ready to use.

Makes 1¼ cup

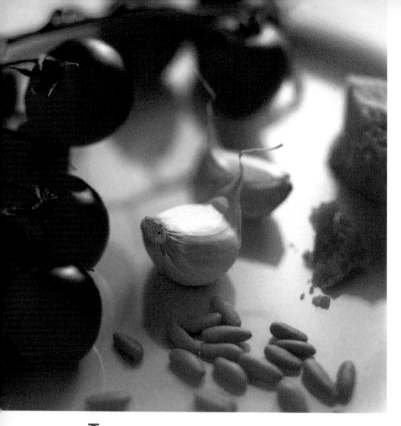

Bring a large pot of salted water to a boil. Add the linguine and cook according to the package directions until it is just tender.

Meanwhile, heat the oil in a large skillet, and sauté the onion and garlic over medium heat until softened. Stir in the roasted tomatoes, tomato sauce, and chicken stock. Simmer for 5 minutes, stirring occasionally.

Drain the linguine thoroughly and transfer it to a warmed serving bowl.

Stir the basil, salt, and pepper into the sauce, remove the skillet from the heat, and pour the sauce over the linguine. Sprinkle with the toasted pine nuts, shaved Parmesan, and fresh basil. Serve immediately.

Serves 4
(Makes 3 cups Roasted Plum Tomato Sauce)

LINGUINE WITH ROASTED PLUM TOMATO SAUCE

This is reminiscent of my mother's spaghetti but without the meatballs. Roasting plum tomatoes lets you satisfy your tomato cravings year-round.

1   POUND LINGUINE

ROASTED PLUM TOMATO SAUCE

1   TABLESPOON OLIVE OIL
1   CUP FINELY CHOPPED ONION
2   TEASPOONS MINCED GARLIC
1   CUP ROASTED PLUM TOMATOES (SEE PAGE 37)
1   CUP TOMATO SAUCE
½   CUP HOMEMADE CHICKEN STOCK OR
      CANNED BROTH
¼   CUP CHOPPED FRESH BASIL LEAVES
½   TEASPOON SALT
¼   TEASPOON GROUND BLACK PEPPER
¼   CUP TOASTED PINE NUTS
      SHAVED PARMESAN CHEESE
      FRESH BASIL LEAVES CUT INTO JULIENNE STRIPS

MOCHA TORTE WITH CRÈME ANGLAISE AND RASPBERRY COULIS

This is a smashing finale to any meal and will satisfy the most discerning chocoholic. I love the idea of a dessert that you don't have to bake—especially one as rich and sensual as this is.

12	OUNCES (2 CUPS) SEMISWEET CHOCOLATE CHIPS
¾	CUP UNSALTED BUTTER
4	LARGE EGGS, SEPARATED
3	TABLESPOONS INSTANT ESPRESSO COFFEE GRANULES DISSOLVED IN 2 TABLESPOONS WATER OR KAHLÚA
2	ENVELOPES (4¼ TEASPOONS) UNFLAVORED GELATIN
¼	CUP COLD WATER
½	TEASPOON CREAM OF TARTAR
⅛	TEASPOON SALT
¾	CUP SUGAR RASPBERRY COULIS (PAGE 164) AND CRÈME ANGLAISE (PAGE 76), OR PRALINE PECAN SAUCE (PAGE 95) AND WHIPPED CREAM

Line a 9 x 5-inch loaf pan with a large piece of plastic wrap, and set it aside.

Melt the chocolate and butter in the top of a double boiler over simmering water. Whisk in the egg yolks and the espresso mixture.

Stir the gelatin into the cold water; let sit 1 minute. Then whisk the gelatin into the mocha mixture and remove it from the heat. Transfer the mocha mixture to a large bowl, and let it cool for about 10 minutes.

Thoroughly wash and dry the top of the double boiler and place it over simmering water. Place the egg whites in the double boiler and beat at high speed with an electric mixer until foamy; add the cream of tartar and salt, and whip at high speed until soft peaks begin to form. Gradually add the sugar, whipping until stiff, but not dry, peaks form.

Fold the egg whites into the cooled mocha mixture, and blend well. Pour the mixture into the prepared pan, cover with plastic wrap, and refrigerate for 4 to 5 hours.

To serve: Invert the loaf pan over a serving plate, and lift off the pan; peel off the plastic wrap. Cut the torte into thin slices, and serve it with Raspberry Coulis and Crème Anglaise or with Praline Pecan Sauce and whipped cream.

Serves 10

a picnic at the beach

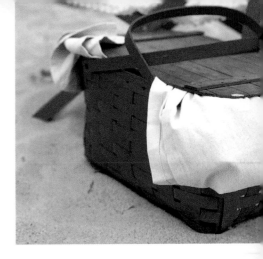

AS A CHILD I longed to live near the ocean (just like Gidget), but growing up in landlocked western Pennsylvania, my only exposure to beach life was via television and the movies. The surfing didn't interest me—it was all that sand, those crashing waves, and the fabulous beach houses! I vowed I would live in one of those beach communities someday.

My first visit to a New York State beach was love at first sight. In the beginning there was Coney Island, then Far Rockaway, and by Jones Beach I was hooked. Modeling assignments took me to various island and coastal locations, which helped deepen my beach obsession, but finally it was the Hamptons on Long Island that sent me over the top and—fast forward— where Dan and I eventually bought a house.

The beach parties I used to read about and see in movies are now steps away from our door: clambakes, lobster grills, sunset suppers, and picnics galore.

Page 44: *Jazmyn Young, our neighbor in Sag Harbor, in the tent the girls made for their party.* Above: *Steve Bagby, Christina Carr, and Rashid Silvera gathered around our makeshift table.* Opposite: *Guest of honor Rashid Silvera.*

When we have house guests and parties, most of our socializing takes place out on the sand. The idea is to keep things casual, but still elegant.

With that in mind, Dan and I decided to have a picnic on the beach for our dear friend Rashid Silvera, who as a fashion model has established a standard for personal style and as an educator has touched the lives of many young students. Rashid, who holds degrees from Harvard Divinity School, teaches psychology and political science at Scarsdale High School in New York's Westchester County.

We chose the Saturday of the weekend Rashid was to be our houseguest, and I invited a number of mutual friends who share our fashion-biz connections. To set a distinct tone in honor of Rashid's fashion savoir-faire, I asked that everyone dress in shades of white and beige.

Asking people to dress a certain way creates a camaraderie among your guests before the party even begins. Having a "dress code" establishes right from the start that each guest is an active participant in the event, each contributing to the whole. It's even an ice-breaker of sorts, in that people have at least *that* in common!

The time—around seven, just before dusk on one of those long summer days when the sun takes forever to set—was chosen for the spectacular light. As for the weather, well, we let that be the unpredictable factor in the equation, adding an air of anticipation to the day.

In keeping with my goal for the party—easy yet elegant—as many preparations as possible were done in advance so I could relax with my guests. With planning, you can reduce the last-minute work to a minimum, allowing you to maintain a pleasant pace and not be totally worn out by the time people start arriving.

Particularly for an outdoor event, make sure the menu has uncomplicated dishes that can be prepared ahead of time. The pound cake I served for dessert can be baked one to two days in advance and then wrapped in several layers of plastic wrap. On the morning of the party I washed and dried the salad greens and then tossed them in a plastic bag before refrigerating them.

That morning I also made the gazpacho, which should chill for a few hours before serving. This is the most labor-intensive dish on the menu, although I find all the peeling

DRESSED TO THRILL

Asking your guests to dress a certain way can make for some surprising interpretations! There are always the standbys: "Dress: Formal" or "Casual Attire." But don't stop there—let your imagination roam a bit.

Theme parties are a good way to encourage your guests' creativity. A Western party would call for cowboy boots, Stetsons, and lots of buckskin fringe. The dress for a luau would consist of Hawaiian shirts, sarongs, and leis, while a '60s soirée would get everyone into love beads, bell-bottoms, and tie-dye.

Another way to sartorially challenge your guests is by requesting that they wear one specific element of dress: Ask everyone to wear a hat, or ask everyone—men included—to show some décolletage. Request your invitees to display the gaudiest tie they can find or to adorn themselves with an outrageous wig.

You could ask that people dress as their favorite Hollywood movie star or a literary character they admire. From the sublime to the ridiculous: invite everyone to come as a cartoon character or as someone from a nursery rhyme. We went to a party once where the guests were asked to come as their favorite building in Manhattan!

Of course you could just leave it up to your guests and insist that they come as they are. Even that might elicit something unexpected!

GRILLING GUIDELINES

There are two basic types of grills: open or covered. One of the most popular of the open grills is the tiny, but highly transportable, hibachi. It's perfect for grilling small amounts of food like hors d'oeuvres or a meal for two. The hibachi is small enough to fit in the trunk of your car and can even be placed in an indoor fireplace to satisfy grill cravings in winter.

The round charcoal-burning kettle grill is another favorite. It is usually equipped with wheels for easy mobility and can be used with or without its cover.

In addition to charcoal grills, there are gas grills and electric grills. Figuring out what your needs are, the types of food you plan to cook on the grill, and what your budget will allow will help you decide which grill is right for you.

You no longer have to go through the wads of crumpled newspaper followed by a multitude of matches, that used to be the routine for getting the charcoal going. My next-door neighbor in Sag Harbor introduced me to the charcoal chimney starter, and I was instantly hooked. These chimneys (actually a foot-high metal cylinder) hold up to four pounds of charcoal briquettes and can be ignited using a single sheet of newspaper and the light of one match. Better still: no more lighter fluid required, eliminating the nasty residue taste it left on food. The coals heat up beautifully, and then you lift the cylinder, letting the hot coals pile up in the grill—and you're ready to cook.

Before you begin to grill, keep these tips in mind:

• Remove the old ashes before you set up the briquettes, so air can circulate around them.

• Be sure the fire has burned down and the coals are covered with a fine gray ash before placing any food on the grill rack.

• Use the best quality charcoal available.

• Food should be at room temperature before it's grilled.

and chopping of the vegetables to be relaxing. If this is not the case with you, there's always a food processor to speed things up.

The gazpacho can be carried in Thermoses, making it easily transportable to any outdoor event. I also toss in some small ice cubes made of tomato juice to help the chill last longer. You could have some cold vodka on hand for those guests who want to give their soup a boost. The best part about this delicious concoction is how easy it is to serve when the time comes. Pour the gazpacho directly from the Thermos into cups, mugs, or glasses—I used acrylic tumblers at my beach party—and let everyone sip away. No spoons necessary; one less detail to bother about.

By the time I finished preparing the salad and the gazpacho, it was time for lunch. This is when you can round up the kids and get them involved in a little party of their own. Again, the point is not to create a fancy affair—it's more about doing something that the children can be involved in.

At lunchtime on the day of the beach party, my stepdaughter, Dana, and three of her friends helped create their own outdoor picnic. First, a special place had to be created, and the girls accomplished this with things they found around the house: a tent fashioned out of some fabric, rope, safety pins, some wooden poles, and colored paper.

The girls scouted out a site near an apple tree on a grassy spot overlooking the water. The poles were

Left and below: *The girls held their own picnic in a tent they made and decorated themselves.* Above: *They used cookie molds to give their sandwiches fun shapes.*

put in the ground, draped with fabric, and then decorated. The finishing touches were the star, crown, cone, and magic ball—and some wild flowers they picked and arranged on a stool.

I had made up batches of tuna and chicken salad so everyone could make their own lunch. The girls were given some cookie molds so they could make cut-out shapes from their sandwiches. This of course delighted them—anything to be able to play with their food! There were also chips and plenty of fruit punch.

Dessert consisted of oversize oatmeal and peanut butter cookies, and then we made some fruit juice pops for a late afternoon snack. Dana and her friends poured the juice into paper cups and put them in the freezer. When they began to freeze we stuck sticks into their centers, and in a short time the kids had homemade popsicles.

After lunch there was a rousing rendition of Quack-A-Dilly-Oh-So, which involved a lot of clapping and giggling, and a spirited session of Operator, where whispered secrets were passed around.

Parties for kids can easily be carried out at the last minute. Dana's tent party not only was fun for them—and for me—but kept the girls from feeling left out as preparations continued for the adult party later that evening.

After lunch and playing with the girls, I returned to the evening's menu and mixed the herb marinade for the vegetables. To good olive oil, salt, and pepper, I added a combination of rosemary, oregano, basil, and thyme (but any assortment of fresh herbs will work). While I had the herbs out, I made the basil vinaigrette dressing for the salad in a glass jar with a tight-fitting lid that I could carry to the picnic later.

In a plastic container I tossed the marinade with the vegetables—red, yellow, and green bell peppers, Japanese baby eggplants, and zucchini—all cut into large pieces. I covered the container with an airtight lid and put it in the refrigerator to marinate. When the time came, the vegetables were transferred directly from the plastic container to the grill.

The only other food preparation I had left to do at this point was to prepare the fresh fruit for the pound cake. I added honey to an assortment of fresh ripe strawberries, blueberries, raspberries, and blackberries, creating a colorful mélange of tastes and textures. When you create a mixture like this, allow enough time for the berries to get to know each other, so by the time you're ready to serve dessert they're on very good terms. The mixture can be refrigerated in a plastic bowl with a lid, ready to be transported to the beach.

Now it was time to get myself ready for my guests' arrival. Whenever you plan a party, make sure you allow for psychological preparation. When things get underway, it's important that you feel refreshed and relaxed rather than frazzled and frenzied. As the host you'll be establishing a tone, and in order to convey one of ease and relaxation, you need to project that yourself. Whether it's a bubble bath, a five-mile run, or a leisurely swim before getting

Opposite: *Alexandra, Dana, Rachel, and Erica playing Quack-A-Dilly-Oh-So.* Above: *Dana passes the secret to Alexandra as they play Operator.*

To avoid broken glass on the beach, I like to use paper plates in wicker holders and acrylic glasses.

fortably could, the party was in motion. By the time our procession to the beach had begun, in fact, the party was already well underway!

To make the trek from my house somewhat stylish and orderly, I had packed everything in the straw baskets I collect, my wicker suitcase, and a big picnic hamper. A favorite old jacquard coverlet, no longer used on the bed, was perfect for bundling things up and carrying them to the beach; later we spread it out on the sand to sit on.

We made a lively procession that evening, laden with food and drink, odds and ends, high spirits and high hopes! No one was daunted by the clouds that had crept in.

I had scouted out a location earlier and had set the grill up and lit the coals, which take about 30 to 40 minutes to get thoroughly heated and covered with a fine gray ash. When the party arrived that evening we were ready to unfold the chairs and mix the drinks. The marinated vegetables and the swordfish steaks were laid out, ready for the grill. I had also brought along some loaves of crusty bread to be sliced thickly, brushed with olive oil, and set on the grill for a few moments—just long enough to toast on both sides—a super-easy appetizer.

Entertaining outdoors adds a degree of adventure in that the weather may cause plans to change at the last minute or, as in this case, in mid-party. As the host, you should be prepared with a contingency plan. My plan was to move the festivities back to the house should the elements fail to cooperate. If you'd prefer that the guests not retreat to

dressed, create the time for this necessary indulgence.

When people began arriving, a little after seven, all the food and party gear was assembled and ready to be transported to the beach. Drinks were offered at the house, but for an event like this, where everything has to be carried to the party site, it's a good idea to keep the selection as simple as possible. I had sparkling water, an assortment of juices, vodka, and white wine on hand, along with plenty of lemon and lime wedges.

With everyone pitching in and carrying as many things as they com-

BEACH STYLE

To individualize a beach site for a party or picnic, make use of things that are easy to carry and that will stand up to the sand and sun.

Large pieces of fabric, blankets, and oversize towels can all be used in a variety of ways. Fabric can cover an unsightly cooler and at the same time help to insulate it from the heat and sunlight. Folding lawn or beach chairs can be transformed by draping lightweight blankets over them to hide wear and tear, change a color, add texture, and provide some cushioning. Use a tablecloth to wrap up plates, bowls, and platters for transport to the beach and then spread it out for a picnic blanket.

Bring along pillows—small ones will do—to sit on or lean against. And for when the sun finally does set, use light sources that will stand up to the ocean breezes. Bamboo torches are good for perimeter lighting, as are candles set in sand-filled paper bags; hurricane lamps are best for close-range illumination.

Scavenging excursions can turn up all sorts of beautiful things to decorate and personalize any picnic spot. We found seashells and pine berries, driftwood and beach grass, all of which can be fashioned into artful arrangements. Stones can be gathered to make decorative borders or simply to use as weights when things get breezy.

For my party we used a couple of good-size rocks to support a large piece of plywood for a makeshift table, establishing a surface to set things on and also serving as a focal point.

the house, have an enclosed porch or the garage prepared to receive them. Chairs and tables and a bar should be set up in advance, as well as decorations to maintain continuity with the original theme of the outdoor party. And, in case the downpour occurs with too little warning, have some towels and dry clothes on hand. Think like a Scout: Be prepared!

It wasn't raining on my party, though, and everyone settled in,

chatting and sipping their drinks. We basked in the glow of the coals as the daylight started to fade. What had been a sandy spot on the beach not long ago had been transformed into a warm convivial place where the fresh salty air mingled with the con-

versation, the waves provided background music, and we continued to ignore the massing clouds.

The swordfish steaks had been marinating in a lime and garlic mixture for about 15 or 20 minutes. (Don't let it sit in the marinade too long or the citrus will begin to cook the fish.) Once on the grill—placed in the middle over the highest heat—a one-inch-thick swordfish steak needs only 4 to 5 minutes on each side.

Grilled meat and chicken are, of course, other options. I chose swordfish because it requires less cooking, making it fast and easy to prepare. Another fish that works beautifully on the grill is tuna, and if you're willing to make a bit more of an effort, seafood brochettes are always a crowd pleaser.

Once the fish was underway it was time to start the vegetables. I arranged them around the perimeter of the grill, where the heat is less intense. (Keep a close eye on the vegetables, for they will cook quite quickly and though you want them to be tender, you don't want them to burn.)

I have always loved food cooked over fire and recall a particular Memorial Day when relatives gathered at my mother's house. A pit was dug in the yard, not far from the grape arbor, and over the course of the day a whole pig cooked slowly. It took time and tending and was quite an undertaking that required patience and not a little skill. Throughout the afternoon people

came and went, stories and jokes were told, and laughter seemed continuous. Roasting the pig was a great excuse to bring everyone together.

I've come to appreciate the finer points of grilling, and I've met more than a few great grill masters, all of whom have my respect. The art of grilling requires perseverance and attentiveness, but this dedication pays off.

When I'm hosting an event, I like to turn over grill duty to some stalwart volunteer so I can stay mobile and keep things running smoothly. There is never any shortage of takers for being keeper of the flame, as I've happily found over the years!

The tableware I had selected for this picnic was real flatware and cloth napkins, and, to avoid broken glass on the beach and for easy transport, I opted for paper plates in wicker holders and acrylic glasses. As we filled our plates with salad and fresh-from-the-grill fish and vegetables, we were too preoccupied to notice the gathering clouds.

A little while later, as we finished eating, the sky opened. We made a dash back to the house—grabbing the berries and the lemon pound cake for our dessert—whooping and hollering the whole way.

Slightly damp but undaunted, we spooned up our dessert, savoring the rich mix of strawberries, blueberries, blackberries, and raspberries with the sweet, lemony cake as we watched the rain fall.

MENU

Tangy Gazpacho

Mixed Green Salad with Basil Vinaigrette

Marinated Grilled Swordfish Steaks

Herb-Marinated Grilled Vegetables

Lemon Pound Cake

White Wine

Vodka and Mixers

Assorted Alcoholic and Nonalcoholic Beers

Sparkling Water

Chilled Plum Wine

Tangy Gazpacho

Originated in Spain, this soup has a peppery taste and is an excellent no-cook option in hot steamy weather. It makes perfect picnic fare transported by Thermos and sipped out of cups. To add an extra kick for a brunch or a summer supper, add a splash of vodka.

3½ CUPS SEEDED PEELED RIPE TOMATOES (ABOUT 2 POUNDS)
1 CUP CHOPPED, SEEDED, PEELED CUCUMBER (½ MEDIUM)
1 CUP CHOPPED RED BELL PEPPER
1 CUP CHOPPED GREEN BELL PEPPER
½ CUP CHOPPED RED ONION
½ CUP CHOPPED CARROTS
¼ CUP CHOPPED CELERY
¼ CUP FRESH CILANTRO LEAVES
1 TEASPOON CHOPPED GARLIC
2 TABLESPOONS OLIVE OIL
2 TABLESPOONS CIDER VINEGAR
1 TABLESPOON FRESH LIME JUICE
½ TEASPOON PAPRIKA
1 TEASPOON SALT
¼ TEASPOON GROUND BLACK PEPPER
¼ TEASPOON GROUND CUMIN
⅛ TEASPOON CAYENNE PEPPER
1½ CUPS TOMATO JUICE
FRESH CILANTRO LEAVES, FOR GARNISH

Place the tomatoes, cucumber, bell peppers, onion, carrots, celery, cilantro leaves, and garlic in a food processor. Add the oil, vinegar, and lime juice. Purée until smooth. Transfer the mixture to a large bowl, and stir in the paprika, salt, black pepper, cumin, cayenne pepper, and tomato juice; blend well. Refrigerate for 2 to 3 hours or until thoroughly chilled. Before serving, garnish with extra cilantro leaves, if desired.

Makes 6 cups (Serves 6)

Marinated Grilled Swordfish Steaks

Swordfish steaks are one of my favorite fish for grilling. They hold up well on the grill and need few, if any, additions to their delicious meaty texture.

4 (8-OUNCE) SWORDFISH STEAKS, ABOUT 1 INCH THICK

MARINADE

½ CUP OLIVE OIL
¼ CUP FRESH LIME JUICE
1 TABLESPOON MINCED GARLIC
½ TEASPOON SALT
½ TEASPOON GROUND BLACK PEPPER

LIME WEDGES, FOR GARNISH

Prepare an outdoor grill. Rinse the swordfish steaks and pat them dry with paper towels.

Mix all the marinade ingredients together in a small bowl. Place the swordfish steaks in a shallow dish or plastic container, and pour the marinade over the fish. Cover and marinate for 15 minutes.

Remove the fish from the marinade and grill it, 4 to 6 inches away from the heat source, for about 5 minutes each side or until the fish flakes easily when tested with a fork. Serve immediately, with lime wedges.

Serves 4

HERB-MARINATED GRILLED VEGETABLES

Vegetables take really well to grilling, whether they are on skewers or placed directly on the grill rack. You can grill them in advance and serve them at room temperature, or you can eat them hot off the fire.

HERB MARINADE

¾ CUP OLIVE OIL

¼ CUP RED WINE VINEGAR

1 TEASPOON CHOPPED FRESH ROSEMARY,
OR ½ TEASPOON DRIED

1 TEASPOON FRESH THYME LEAVES, OR
½ TEASPOON DRIED

1 TEASPOON CHOPPED FRESH BASIL,
OR ½ TEASPOON DRIED

1 TEASPOON CHOPPED FRESH OREGANO,
OR ½ TEASPOON DRIED

1 TABLESPOON MINCED GARLIC

½ TEASPOON SALT

½ TEASPOON GROUND BLACK PEPPER

2 POUNDS ASSORTED VEGETABLES (BELL PEPPERS,
ZUCCHINI, EGGPLANT, ONIONS), LEFT
WHOLE IF SMALL, CUT IN HALF IF LARGE

Whisk together all the marinade ingredients in a small bowl. Arrange the vegetables in a shallow dish or plastic container, pour the marinade over them, cover, and refrigerate for 2 hours.

Prepare a grill.

Remove the vegetables from the marinade (reserve the marinade). Grill the vegetables 6 inches away from the heat source until they are tender, brushing them with the marinade as they cook.

Cooking times will vary according to the vegetable.

Serves 4

LEMON POUND CAKE

This pound cake is the most versatile of desserts and will satisfy a sweet-tooth craving in a second. You can cover it with fruit, chocolate sauce, ice cream, frozen yogurt, whipped cream, or Raspberry Coulis (see page 164). Or you can, and probably will, just eat it by itself!

3	CUPS ALL-PURPOSE FLOUR
1½	TEASPOONS BAKING POWDER
½	TEASPOON SALT
¾	TEASPOON GROUND MACE
1½	CUPS UNSALTED BUTTER, AT ROOM TEMPERATURE
2¼	CUPS SUGAR
6	LARGE EGGS, AT ROOM TEMPERATURE
1	TABLESPOON VANILLA EXTRACT
3–4	TABLESPOONS FRESHLY GRATED LEMON ZEST

Preheat the oven to 325° F. Thoroughly grease a 10-inch tube pan or two 9 x 5-inch loaf pans with nonstick cooking spray or melted butter.

Sift the flour, baking powder, salt, and mace together in a large bowl. In another large bowl, beat the butter and sugar together until light and fluffy. Then beat in the eggs, one at a time, along with the vanilla and lemon zest. Gradually add the flour mixture to the butter mixture, beating well after each addition. Pour the batter into the prepared pan, and bake for 1 hour, or until the center is as solid to the touch as the outer edges.

Let the cake cool in the pan for 10 minutes. Then turn it out onto a wire rack and allow it to cool completely.

Makes one 10-inch tube or two 9 x 5-inch cakes
Serves 8 to 10

a formal dinner for eight

FORMAL CAN BE FUN!

And, with some planning and organization, very manageable. This is the chance to pull out all the stops and use your beautiful things that are too special for everyday. Whether it's family or close friends for whom you want to create a labor of love, or business associates you want to make a good impression on, or a special person you want to honor, you can create a memorable occasion for people to come together to eat and converse.

An occasion like this calls for proper invitations that are either handwritten—in pretty ink, with good penmanship, and on beautiful paper—or commercially printed with a similar attention to detail. The invitations themselves should convey the formality of the event and specify whether or not you are requesting formal attire. Invitations should be mailed three weeks in advance, and you should follow up with

Sherry Bronfman's dining room includes a stunning table with a solid marble top (see page 62). I chose place mats rather than a tablecloth in order to highlight this beautiful surface.

sion and it's small enough that it encourages talking one-on-one.

More so than at most social events, the art of making conversation really comes into play at a formal dinner. Seating arrangements and possible topics of discussion should be carefully thought out. The nature of a sit-down affair is that everyone does sit—a captive audience of whomever they sit next to. It's not necessary to place people together only if they know each other. Sometimes a dinner party can actually be more interesting when people are seated next to those they haven't met. Devising a successful seating arrangement is one of the more creative aspects of planning a formal dinner; I'm particularly gratified when people call me the day after the party to tell me they ended up next to their dream dinner mate.

To arrange the seating when it's time for dinner, you can either direct your guests to the places you have selected or you can have place cards on the table. The first method is slightly trickier and may require a little finesse. I find it's often easier to use place cards, especially when more than eight people are involved.

The place cards can be hand-written, or you can print out some fun ones on a computer. Everyone can have the same type of card or you can individualize them, perhaps to reflect some specific (flattering!) characteristic—which works as a nice ice-breaker as well. Whether they're understated or ornate, the particulars of your event—who is invited, the nature of the occasion—determine the style and tone of the place card you use. For instance, if

a phone call to anyone who hasn't responded a week or so before the party just in case the invitation went astray in the mail.

Since conversation is crucial to a successful dinner party, it's important to invite the right number of people—too many makes conversation confusing and too few often makes it hard to keep flowing. A dinner party with eight guests is ideal; the number isn't so large that it prohibits open discus-

it's a gathering of friends, you need use only their first names, whereas at dinners that include business associates, full names and maybe even titles are in order.

For a strictly formal affair I prefer a simple yet elegant look—unadorned cards with the names beautifully written on them. However, if it's a special occasion, I'll incorporate a visual motif, like having the place cards done in red and green for a Christmas Eve supper, or for a fiftieth anniversary celebration, printed in gold and mounted on mini bottles of Champagne.

Another way of establishing a celebratory tone is selecting music that is appropriate to the event. Recorded music is fine as long as the volume doesn't interfere with people being heard. For a more elaborate effect, live music is wonderful. I was once a guest at a dinner where a harpist played while we ate, and it added a very special element to the evening.

As important as who sits next to whom is what they will sit at: a round table or a square one. My dinner party took place during the Christmas holidays in Sherry Bronfman's dining room. I love the formal lines of the rectangular table, which I decorated festively with Christmas ornaments and seasonal china pieces depicting holiday motifs.

Sherry and I were junior models together and share an interest in community involvement. A patron of the arts and a style-setter when it comes to entertaining in her beautiful townhouse, Sherry has a formal dining room to die for! And she was gracious enough to let me use it, since I don't have a formal dining room in my apartment. Her dining table has a gorgeous marble top, so I used place mats to avoid hiding this unique element with a tablecloth.

To keep the conversation flowing, you can have everyone move to another seat at the end of each course. This is a practice for large groups of 12 or more that enables each guest to meet a few different people throughout the meal, and if you do end up next to a dinner companion with whom you have nothing in common, the entire evening won't be spent trying to find something to talk about.

A formal dinner usually progresses at a leisurely pace, especially if the talk gets really lively. Although you won't want to serve the next course until everyone is finished, if you have a particularly slow eater, gently clearing away the dishes is a subtle reminder that the meal is moving on.

Having coffee and dessert in another room is one more way of letting everyone get up from the table

and talk to someone new. If you don't have the space to do that, give your guests a change of visual venue: use different sets of dishes for each course or alter the lighting as the evening goes on, starting with bright at the beginning to dimmed down and candle-lit as the hour gets later.

And no matter how late it gets to be, coffee is always in order at the end of a formal dinner. If you don't own a silver coffee service, see if you can borrow one, because it really adds a gracious note to your evening.

For a finish to a fine meal only freshly brewed coffee will do. If you are able to, offer cappuccino, espresso, and café au lait. There are some great flavored coffees on the market; sample them to find one that fits in with your menu and coordinates with the dessert. Offer alternatives as well—tea and decaf—for your guests. (If you plan on entertaining with any regularity, I recommend investing in a coffee maker that can make at least eight cups, ideally twelve.) To enrich the experience, serve real cream for those willing to indulge; an interesting variation to the bowl of white granulated sugar is brown sugar cubes stacked on an attractive plate. For tea drinkers have fresh lemon and honey on hand.

You may want to forgo dessert altogether and just serve a selection of chocolates with your coffee. Liqueurs—amaretto, Kahlúa, crème de cacao, and crème de menthe—which can be either sipped separately or poured directly into the coffee, are another sweet way to end the meal.

What time you end is, of course,

DRESSING THE TABLE

Dressing the table is like dressing yourself—both require an attention to detail in order to create the desired overall effect.

Start with the foundations: decide what you'll cover the table with before you place anything on it. It's a good idea to have a basic wardrobe of tablecloths in different colors, textures, and lengths.

Whether you want to go for a frilly, lacy look or a more serviceable white linen covering, don't limit yourself to just tablecloths. You can also use bedspreads or sheets (which come in all sorts of wonderful designs), pieces of fabric, or quilts. For more minimal coverage try a runner down the center of your table or place mats for each setting.

Next come the basics: the dishes, silverware, and glasses. Exactly what you put out will be determined, obviously, by what you'll be eating and drinking and how many courses will be served. Keep in mind that everything does not necessarily have to match perfectly or to be placed just so. For a whimsical effect you can use mismatched dishes that look good together. And you can stack things up: the soup bowl sitting on the salad plate which in turn rests on the dinner plate which itself is on a liner plate.

As for glasses, have plenty of them: one for water and one or two for wine. As long as they're sparkly, smudgeless, and arranged well, they'll look great whether they match or not.

Next think about what I consider the crowning glory of the table: the centerpiece. This may consist of one large arrangement, but you want to guard against anyone's view being obstructed. Keep things either low to the table or raised above eye level. Of course flowers are a favorite, but they're not the only choice. There are any number of possibilities and absolutely no rules, so let your imagination run wild: fruits, flowerpots, ceramics, vegetables, stones, plants, sculpture—whatever! If it looks interesting, try it on the table and see if it works visually.

Then again, you may want to forgo a centerpiece altogether and have something decorative at each setting, like little bouquets of flowers or individual potted plants.

Finally come the accessorizing details, the small but significant touches that can mean the difference between a table that seems to lack something and one that has it all. For example, napkins and napkin rings can transform an ordinary place setting into something truly unique. Collect a variety of napkins to reflect a whole range of looks and moods for your table and mix and match them. Napkin rings come in all shapes and sizes, but you can also use things from around the house to hold the napkins: ribbons, beads, flowers, jewelry, yarn, bow ties. And if you know any neat napkin-folding tricks, this is the time to impress your guests!

Don't forget the candles, a lovely glowing addition to any table. Just keep three things in mind: don't use too many, make sure they're steady, and never, ever use scented candles around food.

related to when you begin. I like to serve cocktails before my dinners, so we can make introductions and everyone can unwind a bit before they sit down to eat together, but I make sure the cocktail period never goes on for more than 45 minutes or so. By then, the conversational juices should be flowing and appetites heightened.

Seven o'clock is a good time to

mashed potatoes (comfort food with an aromatic twist), and sautéed green beans. Dessert was profiterole, served with crème anglaise and chocolate sauce. Everything was arranged on the plates in the kitchen before being served, to maintain a formal tone.

At the start of the meal I served a white zinfandel so as not to compete with the curry. Later I offered a sauvignon blanc and a merlot to comple-

kitchen right off of Sherry Bronfman's dining room that had a refrigerator, stove, and sink, so I was able to keep food chilled, heat dishes up, and rinse things off. This made the logistics of my dinner a lot easier.

Sometimes Dan and I can do all that's required. We'll take turns serving and clearing the dishes so that one of us can stay at the table to help keep the conversation going. A rolling cart can also simplify things—both to bring out the food and to take away dirty dishes—needing only a brisk spin around the table after each course to keep the dinner running smoothly. For anyone who entertains a lot, these mobile units are an excellent investment.

The more details you can attend to in advance, the more relaxed you'll be and the more you will get to enjoy this elegant dinner of your making. For example, well in advance of your party, take stock of your china to be sure nothing is chipped or cracked, inventory your silver, and allow time for any polishing that needs to be done. Have your linen freshly laundered and ironed, and make sure the glassware is polished and smudge-free.

I like to set my table a week or so in advance as a practice run of sorts, to see how everything looks, what's missing, and to decide what I want to add or replace. By sitting in each of the chairs, I can get a clear idea of everyone's vantage point and make sure there is nothing unsightly blocking anyone's view.

The preparation for a meal like this will heighten the enjoyment of an evening that all will remember for a long time to come.

WHEN THEY WON'T GO HOME

Chester Redhead, a friend and a highly respected Harlem dentist, often jokes that the most effective way to end an outdoor party is to keep a reserve of mosquitoes on hand in jars and to release them at the appropriate moment. We always have a good laugh and then try to figure out less drastic actions to take.

If clearing away dishes, emptying ashtrays, and tidying up seem too subtle for your no-end-in-sight crowd, you can always get out the vacuum cleaner and start Hoovering!

Flicking the lights on and off usually conveys that the party is over. And if all else fails, a friend of mine swears by this sure-fire method of clearing people out: Change into your pajamas, brush your teeth, bid everyone goodnight, get into bed, and go to sleep!

---

begin the evening so dinner can be served at eight. The pace you like—perhaps longer pauses between dishes to give people more time to converse—and whether you serve three courses or six will also determine what time the evening ends.

I served four courses at my holiday dinner: to start things off, spicy curried vegetables in flaky puff pastry; next came a salad of winter greens with a hearty balsamic vinaigrette; and for the main course, elegant rosemary roast Cornish hens with a natural cream gravy, garlic

ment the richly herbed Cornish hens.

Of course the tempo of the evening is also determined by how the food is served and by whom. If your budget will allow it, you may want to hire someone to take on all the serving responsibilities so that you can stay at the table and concentrate on your guests.

If it's not possible to hire a server, at the very least enlist the help of someone to hang up coats, help serve food, clear away dishes, refill wine glasses, and just generally keep an eye on things. There was a service

MENU

Curried Vegetables in Puff Pastry

Bitter Greens with Balsamic Vinaigrette

Rosemary Roast Cornish Game Hens

Garlic Mashed Potatoes

Sautéed Green Beans

Profiteroles with Vanilla Ice Cream, Crème Anglaise,

and Chocolate Sauce

White Zinfandel

Sauvignon Blanc

Merlot

CURRIED VEGETABLES IN PUFF PASTRY

You can make bite-size versions of this, or larger-size portions as a first course. The curry revs up the vegetables, and your vegetarian guests will applaud you for this spicy creation.

2	TABLESPOONS OLIVE OIL
1	CUP CHOPPED ONION
1½	CUPS DICED POTATO
2	TEASPOONS MINCED GARLIC
1	TABLESPOON GRATED FRESH GINGER
2	TABLESPOONS CURRY POWDER
1	CUP DICED CARROTS
1	CUP THINLY SLICED CELERY
¾	CUP DICED GREEN BELL PEPPER
¾	CUP DICED MUSHROOMS
¾	CUP DICED GREEN PEAS, FRESH OR FROZEN
¾	CUP DICED ZUCCHINI
¾	CUP CORN, FRESH, CANNED, OR FROZEN
1	TEASPOON SALT
	FRESHLY GROUND PEPPER TO TASTE
1½	POUNDS STORE-BOUGHT PUFF PASTRY
1	LARGE EGG, BEATEN
	SEASONAL SALAD LEAVES, FOR SERVING
	TOMATO WEDGES, FOR GARNISH

Heat the oil in a large skillet and sauté the onion over medium heat until softened. Add the potato, garlic, ginger, and curry powder. Sauté, stirring frequently, for 5 minutes. Add the carrots, celery, peppers, mushrooms, green peas, zucchini, corn, salt and pepper to taste. Cover and cook over low heat for about 15 minutes, or until the vegetables are very tender and the mixture is quite dry. Remove from the heat and let cool.

Preheat the oven to 400° F. Line two large baking sheets with parchment paper.

Divide the pastry into 8 pieces. On a lightly floured surface, roll one piece out to form a circle about 10 inches in diameter. Spoon one-eighth of the curried vegetable mixture into the center, and gather the pastry up to form a turnover, pinching the pastry together to hold it in place. Trim the ragged ends from the top of the pastry turnover. Repeat with the remaining pastry and filling. Use the pastry trimmings to cut out leaf and berry shapes to decorate the turnovers, sticking them on with some of the beaten egg. Brush the turnovers all over with the egg, lift them carefully onto the baking sheet, and bake for 20 to 25 minutes or until the pastry is golden and the filling is heated through.

Serve immediately on salad leaves, garnished with tomato wedges.

Serves 8

ROSEMARY ROAST CORNISH HENS

When I first discovered Cornish hens, my theory about cooking fowl was that if you don't fry it, then you stuff it. And I proceeded to do so with a variety of stuffings. Eventually, though, I came to appreciate this simple and delicious version—now a favorite with my family.

4   CORNISH HENS (ABOUT 1 POUND EACH)

MARINADE

¼   CUP VEGETABLE OIL

½   CUP DRY WHITE WINE

1   MEDIUM ONION, CHOPPED

2   CLOVES GARLIC, MINCED

1   TEASPOON DRIED ROSEMARY

½   TEASPOON SALT

½   TEASPOON GROUND BLACK PEPPER

1   SMALL ONION, QUARTERED

1   LARGE CARROT, QUARTERED

1   RIB CELERY, QUARTERED

4   TABLESPOONS CHOPPED FRESH ROSEMARY,
     OR 2 TABLESPOONS DRIED

4   TABLESPOONS UNSALTED BUTTER, SOFTENED

1   CUP HOMEMADE CHICKEN STOCK
     OR CANNED BROTH

1   CUP DRY WHITE WINE

½   TEASPOON SALT

¼   TEASPOON GROUND BLACK PEPPER

½   CUP HEAVY CREAM

Remove the giblets from the hens. Rinse the hens with cold water and pat them dry with paper towels.

Combine the marinade ingredients in a small bowl. Place the hens in a large self-sealing food storage bag and pour the marinade over them. Close the bag securely and refrigerate for at least 3 hours. Shake the bag once or twice to coat the hens evenly with the marinade.

Preheat the oven to 425° F.

Remove the hens from the plastic bag and pat dry with paper towels. Place 1 piece of onion, carrot, celery, and one fourth of the rosemary in the cavity of each hen. Set the hens, breast up, in a large roasting pan and spread 1 tablespoon butter over each one. Roast for 15 minutes to brown. Reduce the oven temperature to 325°F, and continue roasting for 35 to 45 minutes, or until the juices run clear when the flesh is pierced with a sharp knife. Remove the vegetables and transfer the hens to a serving platter. Keep warm.

Skim most of the fat from the roasting pan, and stir in the stock, wine, salt, and pepper. Bring to a boil, reduce the heat, and simmer for 2 to 3 minutes. Then whisk in the cream and reheat gently. Pour the sauce over the hens or serve it separately.

Serves 4

Bitter Greens with Balsamic Vinaigrette

This is a bold, assertive salad that can stand up to strong flavors and so goes very well with fish or meat. The bitterness of the greens is balanced by the mellow onion and the sweet vinaigrette.

8	CUPS TORN UP MIXED BITTER GREENS (ARUGULA, FRISÉE, WATERCRESS, CHICORY, RADICCHIO, SWISS CHARD)
½	CUP THINLY SLICED RED ONION
⅓	CUP OLIVE OIL
3	TABLESPOONS BALSAMIC VINEGAR
1	TEASPOON DIJON MUSTARD
¼	TEASPOON SALT
¼	TEASPOON GROUND BLACK PEPPER OLIVE TAPENADE (SEE PAGE 119) AND TOMATO SALSA (SEE PAGE 156), FOR GARNISH

Toss the greens with the onion in a large serving bowl. In a small bowl, whisk together the oil, vinegar, mustard, salt, and pepper. Pour the dressing over the greens and serve immediately, garnished with Olive Tapenade and Tomato Salsa, if desired.

Serves 4

Garlic Mashed Potatoes

Who doesn't love mashed potatoes? The original comfort food, they come to the table in many different forms. They're always great with gravy, and herbs and vegetables can add flavor and texture (try red bell peppers, parsley, or corn).

2	POUNDS BAKING POTATOES
1	GARLIC CLOVE
1	BAY LEAF
⅔	CUP MILK OR HEAVY CREAM, HEATED
¼	CUP UNSALTED BUTTER
1	TEASPOON SALT
½	TEASPOON GROUND BLACK PEPPER

Rinse and peel the potatoes, and cut them into equal-size pieces. Bring a large saucepan of salted water to a boil and cook the potatoes, with the garlic clove and bay leaf, until tender. Drain, and remove the garlic and bay leaf. Transfer the potatoes to a mixing bowl and mash them, gradually adding the hot milk, butter, salt, and pepper. Serve immediately.

Serves 4

Variation: Use equal quantities of turnips and potatoes, and cook as described.

PROFITEROLES WITH VANILLA ICE CREAM, CRÈME ANGLAISE, AND CHOCOLATE SAUCE

I developed my profiterole craving at an Italian restaurant in Vienna. They were so heavenly, I always ate mine faster than the ice cream could melt! This version is now my favorite and tastes best with a rich ice cream, although frozen yogurt works well too.

½	CUP WATER
¼	CUP UNSALTED BUTTER
½	CUP ALL-PURPOSE FLOUR
2	LARGE EGGS, BEATEN
1 ⅓	CUPS CRÈME ANGLAISE (RECIPE FOLLOWS)
2 ⅔	CUPS VANILLA ICE CREAM (RECIPE FOLLOWS)
1	CUP CHOCOLATE SAUCE (RECIPE FOLLOWS)

Preheat the oven to 425° F. Grease a large baking sheet.

Combine the water and butter in a medium saucepan and slowly bring to a boil. Remove the pan from the heat and add the flour all at once. Beat thoroughly until the mixture leaves the sides of the pan. Return the pan to low heat to dry the dough, 2 to 3 minutes. Then remove it from the heat and gradually beat in the eggs. The mixture should be quite glossy.

Spoon ¼-cup mounds of the dough, spaced well apart, onto the prepared baking sheet. Bake for 15 minutes. Then reduce the temperature to 375° F and bake for another 30 minutes, until the profiteroles are crisp and golden. Transfer them to a cooling rack. Cut a slit in the side of each profiterole to allow steam to escape, and let them cool completely.

To serve: Spoon about ⅓ cup Crème Anglaise onto each dessert plate. Fill each profiterole with ⅔ cup of the ice cream, and place them in the center of the Crème Anglaise. Pour ¼ cup warm Chocolate Sauce over each profiterole, and serve immediately.

Makes 4 large profiteroles

VANILLA ICE CREAM

1 ½	PINTS GOOD-QUALITY VANILLA ICE CREAM, SOFTENED
2	TEASPOONS VANILLA EXTRACT

Stir the ice cream and vanilla extract together in a large bowl until blended. Refreeze until needed.

Males 1 ½ pints

CHOCOLATE SAUCE

12	OUNCES (2 CUPS) SEMISWEET CHOCOLATE CHIPS
¼	CUP SUGAR
⅔	CUP WATER
1	TABLESPOON DARK CORN SYRUP

In a medium-size saucepan, stir the chocolate, sugar, and water together over low heat until the sugar has dissolved. Bring to a boil, reduce the heat, and simmer for 5 minutes. Cool slightly, and then stir in the corn syrup. Serve warm.

Makes 1 ½ cups

CRÈME ANGLAISE

1   CUP MILK

1   CUP HEAVY CREAM

1   WHOLE VANILLA BEAN

3   LARGE EGG YOLKS

½   CUP SUGAR

1   TABLESPOON CORNSTARCH

Combine the milk, cream, and vanilla bean in a medium-size heavy saucepan. Bring to a boil. Remove the pan from the heat and let the mixture infuse for 30 minutes. Then scrape the seeds from the vanilla bean into the mixture, and discard the bean.

Whisk the egg yolks, sugar, and cornstarch together in a medium-size bowl. Slowly whisk in 1 cup of the warm milk mixture. Return the egg mixture to the pan and bring to a very gentle boil, stirring constantly. Boil for 30 seconds. Then immediately remove the pan from the heat and strain the mixture into a pitcher. Refrigerate until cold.

Makes 2¾ cups

a kwanzaa/christmas buffet

KWANZAA IS A Swahili word that means the "first fruits

of the harvest." It's a spiritual celebration and a way for African-Americans to acknowledge their African roots and family traditions. It was created in 1966 by Dr. Maulana Karenga, who was at that time a professor of Black Studies and a leading theorist of the Black Cultural Movement. Like Christmas, *Kwanzaa* is a time to emphasize and reinforce the ideas of togetherness and unity, bringing together immediate family, relatives, and close friends. And with so many people living in nontraditional and extended families, these holidays are perfect opportunities to celebrate in cross-cultural and inclusive ways.

Recently the celebration of *Kwanzaa* has gained

Page 78: *Dominique and Ashley Sharpton, dressed up for our* Kwanzaa *celebration.* Above: *The earth tones of the mud cloth wall hanging behind me and the glow of the candles in the* kinara *add warmth to the setting.*

increasing popularity. There are many books and articles on the subject and people are attending *Kwanzaa* celebrations in African-American communities around the country. My family and I started to observe certain aspects of *Kwanzaa* three years ago. We have always celebrated Christmas—and continue to do so—but *Kwanzaa,* which lasts from December 26 until January 1, is now also an important part of our holiday celebrations.

By combining and transforming traditions from both Christmas and *Kwanzaa* in my own way, I can im-

bue the holiday season with a personal style that reflects my beliefs. For instance, because I admire the symbolism of the black, red, and green of the *Bendera ya Taifa,* or *Kwanzaa* flag—red for the blood our people shed, green for hope, and black for the faces of our people—I incorporate these colors into my celebration. I use the unity cup as a symbol of striving for unity in the family, nation, and race. We clink our glasses and toast one another, sharing encouraging and inspirational thoughts before we drink our Champagne.

We still exchange gifts at Christmas, but we've also adopted the *Kwanzaan* idea of some things being homemade or handcrafted and ideally having an educational or functional purpose to them. And hanging on the Christmas tree, alongside the traditional bulbs and ornaments, are African gourds and handmade Afrocentric decorations.

It seemed only fitting that an event emphasizing inclusiveness would take place in Clarice Taylor's home. Clarice is like a mom to me—she's had good practice, having played mom to Bill Cosby on *The Cosby Show* for so many seasons! She is part of the extended family that has grown up around me over the years, and has always opened her heart and her home to a wide assortment of family and friends. We met as neighbors while living on Hamilton Terrace and quickly adopted one another. Clarice stepped in after my mother died, filling a large gap with love, advice, and understanding.

I worked out a strategy that would allow Clarice's house to accommo-

NGUZO SABA

(THE SEVEN PRINCIPLES OF KWANZAA)

1. **Umoja** (Unity). To strive for and maintain unity in the family, community, nation, and race.
2. **Kujichagulia** (Self-determination). To define ourselves, name ourselves, create for ourselves, and speak for ourselves instead of being defined, named, created for, and spoken for by others.
3. **Ujima** (Collective work and responsibility). To build and maintain our community together, and to make our sisters' and brothers' problems our problems and solve them together.
4. **Ujamaa** (Cooperative economics). To build and maintain our own stores, shops, and other businesses and to profit from them together.
5. **Nia** (Purpose). To make our collective vocation the building and development of our community in order to restore our people to their traditional greatness.
6. **Kuumba** (Creativity). To do always as much as we can, in the way we can, in order to leave our community more beautiful and beneficial than when we inherited it.
7. **Imani** (Faith). To believe with all our hearts in our people, our parents, our teachers, our leaders, and in the righteousness and victory of our struggle.

THE SEVEN SYMBOLS OF KWANZAA

1. **Mazao** (fruit and vegetables, representing the rewards of collective labor)
2. **Mkeka** (straw place mat, symbolizing tradition)
3. **Kinara** (the candleholder for the seven candles, symbolic of the continental Africans)
4. **Vibunzi** (ears of corn, the number reflecting the number of children in the home)
5. **Zawadi** (gifts, preferably homemade or handcrafted with an educational or functional purpose)
6. **Kikombe cha umoja** (communal unity cup)
7. **Mishumaa saba** (the seven candles—one black, three red, and three green—representing the seven principles of *Kwanzaa*)

date twenty for the buffet-style meal. A buffet really is ideal for a big family celebration because it is informal and allows you a tremendous amount of flexibility—essential when you're dealing with a diverse mix of meat-eaters and vegetarians, family and friends, young and old.

Because the ages of guests at a family get-together can cover a wide spectrum—from toddlers to seniors—it's best to start things at an early hour. And although the meal is an important part of the festivities, you will want to allow time for a number of activities besides eating. For example, this is a time when people can give of themselves—reciting poetry, singing a song, or playing a musical instrument. I scheduled my *Kwanzaa* celebration to begin at four o'clock in the afternoon, to allow time for exchanging gifts, enjoying performances, observing holiday rituals, and of course eating dinner.

Drinks were served as people arrived, and I had set out some things to nibble on—raw vegetables and dips, peanuts, and crackers and cheese. Everyone opened their presents at this time, and the spirited gift exchange worked up our appetites so that we were ready to eat shortly after five.

There are a variety of ways to organize the serving and eating arrangements for a buffet, depending on the number of people you invite and your resources in terms of space, tables, and chairs.

Food can be set out on a sideboard and eaten at the dining room table. Or if you don't have a separate dining area, serve the food in the kitchen—using the kitchen table, counters, and stovetop—and have everyone eat in the living room. No matter where you decide to put the food, keep the traffic flow in mind: Avoid buffet gridlock! Don't set up the buffet in a corner—it will become congested. Place the food in a central location so everyone can move around the table (or along the counter) easily. If that's not possible, divide the food among a number

of locations so guests can move freely from one spot to another.

Second, figure out a way for people to sit and eat comfortably. If you don't have a table that's large enough to accommodate everyone, set up small tables that seat two to four people, or provide tray tables that can be placed wherever they're needed. Even a coffee table can be used for children, who can sit around it on the floor. Seating arrangements can be casual in a gathering of this sort, where everyone is on familiar terms, but don't be so casual that people have to sit and hold their plates on their laps. Lap eating is everyone's least favorite form of dining and should be avoided if at all possible. Get the family involved if you don't have adequate seating: on the invitations ask guests to coffee table. Informal? Yes, but definitely fun!

In fact, because it is a family affair, that informality should extend to the invitations as well. At that time of year I'm sending out holiday cards anyway, so I just extended an invitation to my *Kwanzaa* celebration in a personal note that I enclosed in my cards. This is where I explained what I had planned for

BUFFET STYLE

A buffet is one of the best ways to entertain any size group, from very small to extremely large. A buffet will work any time of day and for any occasion, from a family meal to a formal wedding; from breakfast to a dinner to a midnight dessert party.

Plan a menu that includes foods that can be served at room temperature and that will hold up well as they sit out on your buffet table.

Cover your buffet table with something that can stand up to spills and stains, for buffets can sometimes be messy as people help themselves. Instead of the usual flower arrangement, use herbs, vegetables, fruits, and edible flowers to decorate your table.

Fruits and vegetables can also be fashioned into natural but elegant containers for serving food or creating centerpieces.

Be sure to position the serving table or tables for easy access. Do a walk-through before the party to gauge traffic flow and determine how to space the food so people can move smoothly as they fill their plates. You may also decide to have a combination of self-serve and servers who can assist in certain things like carving the meat. For large buffet parties you may want to have separate tables with a different food on each one—fish on one, meat on another, salads on another, and so on. This system is also helpful in maintaining traffic flow.

Dining table arrangements should also be decided beforehand. I like to set the tables ahead of time with glasses, napkins, and silverware so guests can concentrate on getting their food. Or you can roll the silverware in cloth napkins and have these individual place settings available at the end of the food line or on a side table where other necessary items like condiments, dressings, and beverages can also be placed.

Traditional African patterns are used in the fabric of the place mats and napkins. The napkin rings and the wooden bowl are African.

B.Y.O.C. (Bring Your Own Chairs)!

At my buffet all the food was set out on the large table in the dining room, which the guests moved around clockwise, and then everyone was directed toward two rooms off the dining room. Eight adults sat at a round table in the sunroom; in the living room eight adults sat at two card tables and the four children sat on the floor around the the event and asked the invitee to consider what she or he would like to contribute in terms of a cultural exchange. As people responded, I kept track of what each guest would do: sing, dance, recite, or act. To get into the spirit of things, I encouraged everyone to wear something African, such as kente cloth or mud cloth (a cloth dyed in earth tones and exclusive to Africa), or to use the red, green, and black of the flag as accents.

These motifs and colors can be incorporated into the general decor, such as a kente cloth table runner or a wall hanging made from mud cloth. For my event, I used a lot of warm earth tones and bright-colored accents. In the table centerpiece wheat symbolized the harvest and the seven candles were black, red, and green. *Mazao*—fruit and vegetables—is one of the symbols of *Kwanzaa,* and it can take the form of one big beautiful centerpiece or small decorations at each place setting that will eventually be eaten as well.

Food to be served at room temperature should be set out first. Cold dishes can be brought out next and placed on ice, or in the case of a salad, be put out in containers that have been chilled beforehand. And at the last possible moment—while the steam is still rising from them—bring the hot foods out on platters and in bowls. (Keep in mind that you are going to need several serving platters and large bowls, so arrange in advance to borrow some if necessary. I had asked everyone to bring either a bowl or a platter and we actually ended up with too many—but better too many than too few.)

You could set up the whole buffet at once, keeping food hot with chafing dishes or electric trays, but I don't recommend them for such an informal gathering. I think they have an institutional feel to them and don't belong in a family get-together. Besides, bringing food out in stages builds anticipation, as everyone watches to see what will appear next.

The food I chose for my *Kwanzaa* buffet included dishes from a variety of places that reflected our African-American cultural heritage. There were traditional southern dishes like corn bread and sautéed greens (chopped collard and mustard greens, and kale sautéed in olive oil and garlic), and a West Indian–influenced dish of jerk-spiced duck. For those who found the duck too spicy I had fried whiting.

There was ginger beer from

Jamaica for the teetotalers, and Red Stripe beer and Champagne punch for the rest. Clarice served the punch from a small fountain that was all lit up and very festive! Whether or not you have a fountain, it's easy to make a bubbly, colorful punch that simply consists of bright juices like orange and cranberry, with Champagne to taste, and some Triple Sec to top it off.

Dessert was potluck and every-one brought their specialties. There were cakes from family recipes, homemade ice cream, and fresh-baked cookies that the children had decorated. My contribution was sweet potato pecan pie—one of my signature dishes—which can be served at room temperature or piping hot and is guaranteed to disappear.

But before we brought out the desserts everyone, including the children, helped to clear the table. Some people set up an assembly line in the kitchen to wash and dry the dishes while others helped to wrap up the leftovers. Then the desserts were placed on the dining room table, and on the sideboard I set up a coffee urn along with cups, saucers, cream, and sugar. There was tea and hot chocolate for the kids.

With everyone pitching in we were ready in no time to start eating our desserts and to prepare for the evening's entertainment. We all felt relaxed and well fed, and although there was a little performance anxiety in the air, for the most part everyone was eager to get up and show off!

That night proved that food can be an inspiration, for there were some truly memorable acts, including a magic trick that went awry (the rabbit escaped!) and a hilarious Moms Mabley imitation courtesy of Clarice. Songs were sung, by me for one (I sang "If You Believe" from "The Wiz"), jokes told, and ivories tickled. It was a wonderful finale to a night shared with family and friends.

MENU

Black-Eyed Pea Soup with Smoked Turkey

Jalapeño Corn Bread

Warm Mixed Greens Salad

Cornmeal Pan-Fried Whiting

Jerk Duckling

Banana Hash

Sweet Potato Pie with Praline Pecan Sauce

Ice Cream

Holiday Cookies

Champagne Punch

Red Stripe Beer

Ginger Beer

Non-Alcoholic Punch

Coffee, Herbal Tea, Hot Chocolate

BLACK-EYED PEA SOUP WITH SMOKED TURKEY

Black-eyed peas are actually beans. They're a mainstay on many New Year's Day menus where they're thought to bring good luck.

1 ¼	CUPS DRIED BLACK-EYED PEAS (ABOUT 10 OUNCES)
2	TABLESPOONS VEGETABLE OIL
1	LARGE CHOPPED ONION
1	TEASPOON MINCED GARLIC
1	CUP CHOPPED GREEN BELL PEPPER
5	CUPS HOMEMADE CHICKEN STOCK OR CANNED BROTH
1	BAY LEAF
1	TEASPOON SALT
¼	TEASPOON DRIED RED PEPPER FLAKES
¾	CUP DICED SMOKED TURKEY
6	TEASPOONS SOUR CREAM (OPTIONAL) FRESH CILANTRO SPRIGS, FOR GARNISH

Place the black-eyed peas in a large bowl and cover them with cold water. Let them soak overnight.

Drain the peas, rinse them thoroughly, and set them aside to drain again. Heat the oil in a large saucepan over medium-high heat, and sauté the onions and garlic until softened. Add the peas, bell pepper, chicken stock, bay leaf, salt, and red pepper flakes. Cover and bring to a boil. Then reduce the heat and simmer for 1 hour or until the beans are tender. Stir in the smoked turkey and simmer for another 15 minutes.

Remove the bay leaf, and top each serving with a teaspoon of sour cream and a sprig of cilantro, if desired.

Makes about 6 cups (Serves 6)

Note: To turn this soup into a side dish, use 2 cups of chicken stock and delete the sour cream. Makes about 4 cups.

JALAPEÑO CORNBREAD

I never saw cornbread baked in anything but a
black iron skillet when I was young, and that's
how I cook it to this day. You can jazz it up with
a variety of things, including jalapeño or green
bell peppers, which add color, create texture,
and give a southwestern flavor.

When I want to serve this cornbread at a
buffet, I often make muffins because they're
easier to handle when you have a large crowd.
This recipe will make 12 muffins.

2	CUPS YELLOW CORNMEAL
1	CUP ALL-PURPOSE FLOUR
1½	TABLESPOONS BAKING POWDER
1½	TEASPOONS SALT
2	TABLESPOONS DARK BROWN SUGAR
3	LARGE EGGS
1⅓	CUPS MILK
½	CUP UNSALTED BUTTER, MELTED
1	CUP SWEET CORN KERNELS, CANNED (DRAINED) OR FROZEN (THAWED)
½	CUP GRATED CHEDDAR CHEESE
½	CUP GRATED CARROTS
½	CUP GRATED ONION
¼	CUP FINELY CHOPPED FRESH JALAPEÑO PEPPER

Preheat the oven to 400° F. Grease a 10-inch
cast-iron skillet.

In a large bowl, stir together the cornmeal,
flour, baking powder, salt, and brown sugar.
Whisk the eggs, milk, and melted butter in a
medium-size bowl, and stir this into the dry
ingredients. Add the corn, cheese, carrots,
onion, and jalapeño pepper, and stir to
thoroughly combine.

Pour the batter into the skillet and bake for
30 to 35 minutes, until a toothpick inserted in
the center comes out clean. Cut into pieces and
serve from the skillet.

Makes 8 large pieces

Variation: Divide the batter among 24 muffin
cups and bake for 15 to 18 minutes, until the
muffins are well risen and a toothpick inserted
in the center comes out clean. Transfer to a
wire rack to cool.

Rinse the fillets and pat them dry with paper towels.

Mix the cornmeal, flour, salt, paprika, and pepper together in a shallow dish or plastic container. Pour the milk into a shallow dish. Dip the fillets into the milk and then into the cornmeal mixture, coating them well and shaking off any excess.

Heat half the butter in a large skillet over high heat, and fry two of the fillets for about 3 minutes on each side, or until the fish flakes easily when tested with a fork. Transfer the fillets to a serving platter and keep warm. Repeat with the remaining butter and fillets. Serve immediately, with Tartar Sauce and fresh lemon wedges.

Serves 4

TARTAR SAUCE

1	CUP MAYONNAISE
2	TABLESPOONS FINELY CHOPPED RED ONION
2	TABLESPOONS FINELY CHOPPED CELERY
2	TABLESPOONS FINELY CHOPPED TINY GHERKINS (CORNICHONS)
1	TABLESPOON GHERKIN JUICE FROM THE JAR
1/8	TEASPOON CHOPPED FRESH DILL
	PINCH OF CAYENNE PEPPER
	FEW DROPS OF TABASCO SAUCE
	FEW DROPS OF WORCESTERSHIRE SAUCE

Mix all the ingredients thoroughly in a medium-size bowl, and chill until ready to serve.

Makes about 1¼ cups

CORNMEAL PAN-FRIED WHITING

This is the only fish I can remember having as a child. To this day, friends of mine still remember my mother's fried whiting. This dish is delicious served along with Spicy Coleslaw (see page 114).

4	(8-OUNCE) WHITING FILLETS
1	CUP YELLOW CORNMEAL
1/4	CUP ALL-PURPOSE FLOUR
1	TEASPOON SALT
1/2	TEASPOON PAPRIKA
1/4	TEASPOON GROUND BLACK PEPPER
3/4	CUP MILK
6	TABLESPOONS UNSALTED BUTTER
	TARTAR SAUCE (RECIPE FOLLOWS)
	LEMON WEDGES

WARM MIXED GREENS SALAD

This tasty salad can be served as an appetizer, an entrée, or a side dish. I particularly like to combine beet tops, Swiss chard, radicchio, cabbage, frisée, and watercress.

- 2 TABLESPOONS OLIVE OIL, TOASTED SESAME OIL, OR BACON DRIPPINGS
- 2 GARLIC CLOVES (OR TO TASTE), THINLY SLICED
- 8 CUPS CHOPPED GREENS (AT LEAST THREE TYPES: KALE, SWISS CHARD, RADICCHIO, BEET TOPS, WATERCRESS, FRISÉE, SORREL, CABBAGE)
- ½ TEASPOON SALT
- ¼ TEASPOON GROUND BLACK PEPPER CARAMELIZED ONIONS, SAUTÉED BELL PEPPERS, SHREDDED CHEESE, CRUMBLED BACON BITS, OR SLICED HARD-COOKED EGGS, FOR GARNISH

Heat the oil in a large skillet and sauté the garlic over medium-low heat for 1 minute. Add the heartier greens, such as kale, which need a longer cooking time. Sauté for 1 minute, tossing them around in the pan constantly. Add the remaining greens and sauté for another minute or just until wilted. Sprinkle with the salt and pepper, and serve immediately, garnished with caramelized onions, sautéed bell peppers, cheese, bacon bits, or hard-cooked eggs.

Serves 4

JERK DUCKLING

The first time I tasted jerk seasoning was in Jamaica—at a roadside stand where we stopped for jerk chicken. I loved it! Back in New York, at the restaurant Vernon's Jerk Paradise, I found their famous sauce to be an inspiration for me to create my own version. This sauce can be used for chicken, meat, fish, or even vegetables.

2   DUCKS (5 TO 6 POUNDS EACH), CUT IN HALF,
    BACKBONE REMOVED
¼   CUP VEGETABLE OIL
1   RECIPE JERK SEASONING (RECIPE FOLLOWS)
2   CUPS HOMEMADE CHICKEN STOCK OR
    CANNED BROTH

Rinse the ducks with cold water and pat them dry with paper towels. Place them in a large shallow dish or plastic container and refrigerate, uncovered, overnight. Brush the ducks with the oil. Spread 2 tablespoons of the Jerk Seasoning over each duck half, cover, and marinate in the refrigerator for 48 hours, turning occasionally.

Preheat the oven to 500° F.

Place the ducks in a large roasting pan. Prick the skin. Roast for 20 minutes, then reduce the oven temperature to 350° F. Continue roasting for 15 to 20 minutes per pound, or until the skin is crispy and the meat is cooked through, basting occasionally.

Transfer the ducks to a serving platter and keep warm.

Add the remaining Jerk Seasoning to a medium-size saucepan, along with the chicken stock. Bring to a boil, reduce the heat, and simmer for 5 minutes. Pour the sauce over the ducks or serve it separately.

Serves 2

JERK SEASONING

1   CUP COARSELY CHOPPED SCALLIONS
1   COARSELY CHOPPED DRIED SCOTCH BONNET
    CHILE PEPPER OR OTHER HOT CHILE PEPPER
1   TABLESPOON CHOPPED FRESH GINGER
2   GARLIC CLOVES
¼   CUP FRESH LIME JUICE
2   TABLESPOONS VEGETABLE OIL
2   TABLESPOONS FRESH CILANTRO LEAVES
2   TEASPOONS FRESH THYME LEAVES
1   TEASPOON GROUND ALLSPICE
½   TEASPOON GROUND NUTMEG
½   TEASPOON GROUND CINNAMON
1   TEASPOON SALT

Place all the ingredients in the bowl of a food processor, and process until a smooth paste forms. Transfer the seasoning to a container with a tightly fitting lid. Use immediately, or cover and refrigerate for up to a week.

Makes about ¾ cup

BANANA HASH

I call this a "banana" hash because of its brilliant yellow color, but it's a ripe plantain that is the key ingredient.

2 TABLESPOONS UNSALTED BUTTER

1 CUP CHOPPED RED BELL PEPPER

1 CUP CHOPPED SCALLIONS

2 CUPS CHOPPED PLANTAINS (ABOUT 2 MEDIUM)

$\frac{1}{2}$ TEASPOON SALT

$\frac{1}{4}$ TEASPOON GROUND BLACK PEPPER

Melt the butter in a large skillet and add the bell pepper. Sauté for 2 minutes over medium heat, then add the scallions and plantains. Continue to sauté for 10 minutes, or until the plantains are soft. Stir in the salt and black pepper, and serve immediately.

Makes about 3$^{1}/_{2}$ cups

Sweet Potato Pie with Praline Pecan Sauce

Sweet potatoes are often thought of as a humble food, but there is nothing homely about this elegant dessert. My mother's version of this pie called for a traditional white flour crust; I've added spices for extra flavor.

CRUST

1¼	CUPS ALL-PURPOSE FLOUR
3	TABLESPOONS SUGAR
¼	TEASPOON SALT
¼	TEASPOON BAKING POWDER
1	TEASPOON GROUND NUTMEG
1	TEASPOON GROUND CLOVES
1¼	TEASPOON GROUND CINNAMON
½	CUP UNSALTED BUTTER, CHILLED
1	LARGE EGG, LIGHTLY BEATEN
2	TABLESPOONS ICE WATER

NUT MIXTURE

1	CUP FINELY GROUND PECANS
1	TABLESPOON LIGHT CORN SYRUP
1	TABLESPOON UNSALTED BUTTER, MELTED

FILLING

2	CUPS MASHED COOKED SWEET POTATOES (ABOUT 1 POUND SWEET POTATOES)
2	LARGE EGGS, LIGHTLY BEATEN
¼	CUP GRANULATED SUGAR
½	CUP HEAVY CREAM
¼	CUP UNSALTED BUTTER, MELTED
3	TABLESPOONS ALL-PURPOSE FLOUR
2	TABLESPOONS BRANDY
1½	TEASPOONS GROUND CINNAMON
1¼	TEASPOONS GROUND NUTMEG
½	TEASPOON GROUND ALLSPICE
1	TEASPOON VANILLA
⅓	CUP PECAN HALVES

PRALINE PECAN SAUCE (RECIPE FOLLOWS)
WHIPPED CREAM

Prepare the dough for the crust: Stir the flour, sugar, salt, baking powder, and spices together in a large bowl. Using two knives or a pastry blender, cut in the butter until the mixture resembles coarse crumbs. Stir in the egg until well moistened. Stir in the ice water until a dough forms. Wrap in plastic wrap and chill for about 1 hour.

Meanwhile, preheat the oven to 375° F.

Stir the ingredients for the nut mixture in a small bowl, and set aside. In a large bowl (or food processor bowl), beat together all the ingredients for the filling until well blended. Set aside.

Roll the dough out on a floured surface to form a 12-inch circle, and use it to line a 10-inch fluted removable-bottom tart pan. Trim the edges of the dough with a sharp knife. Spread the nut mixture evenly over the bottom, and then pour in the sweet potato mixture. Decorate with the pecan halves. Bake for about 1 hour, until the filling is well risen and set. Transfer to a wire rack to cool.

Serve with Praline Pecan Sauce and whipped cream.

Makes one 10-inch pie (Serves 8 to 10)

Note: This mixture can also be used to make four 4½-inch individual pies. Bake for 35 to 40 minutes.

PRALINE PECAN SAUCE

2	TEASPOONS UNSALTED BUTTER
¼	CUP SUGAR
1¼	CUPS HEAVY CREAM
½	CUP FINELY CHOPPED PECANS, TOASTED

Melt the butter in a medium-size heavy saucepan. Add the sugar and cook over low heat, stirring, until the sugar has dissolved and browned. Stir in the cream and pecans and cook over medium-low heat for 30 minutes, stirring often. Cool slightly before serving.

Makes about 1¼ cups

THE RECIPES

appetizers

HERBED ONION TART

This rich herb-infused tart elevates the lowly onion to lofty heights. Try using Vidalia or another sweet onion of your choice. For a different presentation, you can make small tarts for individual servings.

PIE CRUST

1 ½	CUPS ALL-PURPOSE FLOUR
¼	TEASPOON SALT
3	TABLESPOONS COLD UNSALTED BUTTER
3	TABLESPOONS COLD SHORTENING
3 TO 4	TABLESPOONS COLD WATER

FILLING

2	TABLESPOONS UNSALTED BUTTER
2	CUPS THINLY SLICED ONIONS
1	TABLESPOON ALL-PURPOSE FLOUR
¾	CUP LIGHT CREAM
¾	CUP SOUR CREAM
2	LARGE EGGS, LIGHTLY BEATEN
1	TABLESPOON MINCED MIXED FRESH HERBS, SUCH AS BASIL AND OREGANO
¾	TEASPOON SALT
½	TEASPOON GROUND BLACK PEPPER

Prepare the pie crust: Combine the flour and salt in a medium-size bowl. Using a pastry blender or two knives, cut in the butter and shortening until the mixture resembles coarse crumbs. Stir in just enough cold water to form a dough. Wrap the dough in plastic wrap and chill it for 30 minutes.

Preheat the oven to 400° F.

Roll out the dough on a lightly floured surface to form a 10-inch circle. Invert a 9-inch pie plate on top of dough and cut a clean circle. Line pie plate with the pastry. Prick the bottom with a fork, and line the pastry with waxed paper and pie weights or dried beans. Bake for 12 minutes. Transfer the plate with crust to a wire rack, and remove the pie weights and waxed paper. (Leave the oven on.)

Make the filling: Melt the butter in a large skillet and sauté the onions until softened. Stir in the flour and cook for 1 minute. Then remove from the heat and stir in the light cream, sour cream, beaten eggs, herbs, salt, and pepper. Pour this mixture into the pie shell and bake for 10 minutes. Reduce the heat to 350° F and bake for another 30 minutes, or until the filling is set and golden brown.

Makes one 9-inch tart

SALMON TARTARE

My fondness for Japanese sushi and sashimi is well satisfied with this dish, and I love to order it when we dine at Café des Artistes, a favorite Manhattan eatery of Dan's and mine.

1	POUND FRESH SALMON FILLET, MINCED
½	CUP FINELY CHOPPED RED ONION
1	TEASPOON MINCED GARLIC
2	TEASPOONS CHOPPED FRESH DILL
1	TABLESPOON FRESH LEMON JUICE
½	TEASPOON SALT
½	TEASPOON GROUND BLACK PEPPER
1	TABLESPOON COARSE-GRAIN MUSTARD (OPTIONAL)
1	TABLESPOON COGNAC (OPTIONAL)
1	TABLESPOON OLIVE OIL
	BELGIAN ENDIVE LEAVES, FOR SERVING
	FRESH RADISH STRIPS, FOR GARNISH
	FRESH DILL SPRIGS, FOR GARNISH

Mix all the ingredients together in a large bowl. Serve immediately on a bed of endive leaves, garnished with radish strips and dill sprigs.

Makes about 2 cups

CAJUN CATFISH FINGERS

When I was growing up, catfish were thought of as scavenger fish that, although tasty, weren't anything special. Today's farm-raised catfish have swum their way into mainstream acceptance, and the popularity of these fingers is the proof!

VEGETABLE OIL FOR DEEP-FRYING
2 LARGE EGGS, BEATEN
½ TEASPOON GARLIC POWDER
½ TEASPOON OLD BAY SEASONING
1 TEASPOON WORCESTERSHIRE SAUCE
⅛ TEASPOON TABASCO SAUCE
⅛ TEASPOON DRIED OREGANO
⅛ TEASPOON DRIED THYME
⅛ TEASPOON GROUND BLACK PEPPER
¾ CUP YELLOW CORNMEAL
¼ TEASPOON SALT
1½ POUNDS CATFISH FILLETS, CUT INTO 1-INCH-WIDE STRIPS
SPICY CAJUN DIP (RECIPE FOLLOWS)

Heat the oil to 350° F in a deep skillet or electric fryer.

In a medium-size bowl, whisk together the eggs, garlic powder, Old Bay Seasoning, Worcestershire, Tabasco, oregano, thyme, and black pepper. Mix the cornmeal and salt together in a shallow dish. Dip the catfish strips into the egg mixture and then into the cornmeal mixture to thoroughly coat them.

Fry the fish fingers for about 5 minutes or until golden brown. Remove them with a slotted spoon and drain on paper towels.

Serve immediately, with Spicy Cajun Dip alongside.

Makes about 25 pieces

SPICY CAJUN DIP

½ CUP MAYONNAISE
½ CUP SOUR CREAM
2 TABLESPOONS FRESH LEMON JUICE
½ TEASPOON PAPRIKA
½ TEASPOON GARLIC POWDER
½ TEASPOON CHOPPED FRESH OREGANO
½ TEASPOON CHOPPED FRESH THYME
½ TEASPOON CHOPPED FRESH BASIL
¼ TEASPOON CAYENNE PEPPER
½ TEASPOON GROUND BLACK PEPPER
¼ TEASPOON SALT

Mix together all the ingredients in a small bowl. Cover and refrigerate for at least 2 hours for the flavors to develop before serving with the catfish fingers.

Makes 1 cup

CHITTERLINGS IN PUFF PASTRY

Chitterlings don't often turn up these days. To prevent their falling by the wayside, I created this unusual hors d'oeuvre for special occasions with friends who are familiar with and appreciate this delicacy.

4 CUPS COOKED CHITTERLINGS (SEE PAGE 146)
1½ POUNDS STORE-BOUGHT PUFF PASTRY
1 LARGE EGG, BEATEN

Follow the instructions for Curried Vegetables in Puff Pastry on page 70, using one-eighth of the cooked chitterlings mixture per turnover.

Serves 8

soups

CHILLED MIXED MELON SOUP

Until I tasted this light, refreshing soup, most of the melon I had consumed had been "as is"—scooped from the rind. Use only the ripest, juiciest melons you can find. Cantaloupe halves make an elegant soup bowl. This also works as a quick breakfast drink or healthy midday snack.

3 CUPS WATERMELON, CUT INTO 1-INCH CHUNKS

2 CUPS CANTALOUPE MELON, CUT INTO 1-INCH CHUNKS

2 CUPS HONEYDEW MELON, CUT INTO 1-INCH CHUNKS

¼ CUP LOOSELY PACKED FRESH MINT LEAVES

1 TEASPOON GRATED FRESH GINGER

1 TABLESPOON CRÈME DE MENTHE OR MIDORI HOLLOWED-OUT MELON HALVES, FOR SERVING (OPTIONAL)

FRESH MINT SPRIGS, FOR GARNISH

Place the watermelon, cantaloupe, and honeydew in a blender or food processor. Add the mint leaves and grated ginger, and process until smooth. Pour into a container, stir in the crème de menthe, and refrigerate for at least 1 hour or until thoroughly chilled. Serve in melon shells and garnish with sprigs of fresh mint, if desired.

Makes 6 cups (Serves 4)

Variation: For a creamier soup, stir in 1 cup low-fat buttermilk or plain yogurt.

HENRY'S CHICKEN SOUP

I got this recipe from my chef, Henry Chung, who is Chinese and has also lived in India. Simple to prepare, it's guaranteed to chase away the blues. If you want to make a meal of it, add some vermicelli, rice, or orzo.

4 CUPS HOMEMADE CHICKEN STOCK OR CANNED BROTH

8 OUNCES BONELESS SKINLESS CHICKEN BREAST, CUT INTO ¼-INCH-WIDE STRIPS (ABOUT 1⅓ CUPS)

1 CUP SLICED MUSHROOMS (PREFERABLY OYSTER MUSHROOMS)

1 CUP WATERCRESS LEAVES, LARGE STALKS REMOVED

2 CUPS COOKED RICE OR PASTA (OPTIONAL)

½ TEASPOON SALT

¼ TEASPOON GROUND BLACK PEPPER

Combine the chicken stock, chicken strips, and mushrooms in a large saucepan. Cover and bring to a boil. Then reduce the heat and simmer for 15 minutes or until the chicken and mushrooms are tender. Stir in the watercress, and the rice or pasta if you're using it and the salt and pepper. Cook just until the watercress has wilted and the rice or pasta has heated through, about 2 minutes. Serve immediately.

Makes about 5¼ cups without the rice or pasta (Serves 4)

Mom's Vegetable Soup

I loved watching my mother make this soup, humming to herself as she casually chopped away and then transformed the piles of cut-up vegetables into a heavenly fragrant brew. Of course in those days, the base of the soup was a soup bone from our local butcher. You can make this soup with any of the homemade stocks listed below, or even with a canned broth.

- 2 TABLESPOONS VEGETABLE OIL
- 1 CUP CHOPPED ONION
- 1 CUP SLICED CARROTS
- ½ CUP CHOPPED CELERY
- 3 CUPS HOMEMADE VEGETABLE, CHICKEN, OR BEEF STOCK, OR CANNED BROTH
- 2 CUPS CUBED PEELED POTATOES
- 1 CUP FRESH OR FROZEN SWEET CORN KERNELS
- 1 CUP CHOPPED PEELED RIPE TOMATOES (OR CANNED PLUM TOMATOES, DRAINED)
- 2 BAY LEAVES
- 1 SPRIG FRESH THYME, OR ½ TEASPOON DRIED
- 1 TEASPOON SALT
- ¼ TEASPOON GROUND BLACK PEPPER
  DRIED RED PEPPER FLAKES TO TASTE (OPTIONAL)
- 2 TABLESPOONS CHOPPED FRESH PARSLEY

Heat the oil in a large saucepan. Add the onion, carrots, and celery, and sauté over medium heat until softened. Stir in the stock, potatoes, corn, tomatoes, bay leaves, thyme, salt, black pepper, and red pepper flakes if you're using them. Cover, bring to a boil, and then reduce the heat. Simmer for 30 minutes or until the vegetables are tender. Remove the bay leaves, stir in the parsley, and serve piping hot.

Makes 6 cups (Serves 4)

Berry Berry Soup

As a kid I loved picking the berries that grew wild near my house, and I recall well the feeling of accomplishment when I came home with a pailful of fruit. This cool summer treat is super-easy to make, and if you're not near the wild ones, unsweetened frozen berries will work fine.

- 5 CUPS MIXED BERRIES (STRAWBERRIES, RASP-BERRIES, BLUEBERRIES, BLACKBERRIES)
- 2 CUPS CANNED COCONUT MILK
- ¼ CUP HONEY OR SUGAR (OR TO TASTE)
  WHOLE BERRIES, FOR GARNISH

Place the berries, coconut milk, and honey or sugar in a blender or food processor, and purée until smooth. Pour into a container and chill before serving. Serve garnished with whole berries, if desired.

Makes 4 cups (Serves 4)

BLACK BEAN SOUP WITH ANDOUILLE SAUSAGE AND SOUR CREAM

It wasn't until I moved to New York that I was introduced to Cuban cuisine, and it was at the well-known Victor's Cafe on the Upper West Side that I first tasted black bean soup. Where had it been all my life? For a vegetarian alternative, leave out the sausage and use vegetable stock.

1 ¼	CUPS DRIED BLACK BEANS (ABOUT 8 OUNCES)
2	TABLESPOONS OLIVE OIL
1	CUP CHOPPED ONION
1	TEASPOON MINCED GARLIC
5	CUPS HOMEMADE CHICKEN STOCK OR CANNED BROTH
1	BAY LEAF
1	TEASPOON GROUND CUMIN
1	TEASPOON SALT
½	TEASPOON GROUND BLACK PEPPER
¾	CUP SLICED ANDOUILLE SAUSAGE
1	CUP DICED ZUCCHINI
2	TABLESPOONS DRY SHERRY
1	TABLESPOON FRESH LEMON JUICE
½	TEASPOON TABASCO SAUCE (OR TO TASTE)
6	TABLESPOONS SOUR CREAM, FOR GARNISH
	CHOPPED FRESH PARSLEY, FOR GARNISH

Place the beans in a large bowl and cover them with cold water. Let the beans soak overnight.

Drain the beans, rinse them thoroughly, and set them aside to drain again. Heat the oil in a large saucepan over medium-high heat, and sauté the onion and garlic until softened. Stir in the beans, chicken stock, bay leaf, cumin, salt, and pepper. Cover and bring to a boil. Then reduce the heat and simmer for 1 hour or until the beans are soft, stirring occasionally.

Lightly sauté the sausage slices in a medium-size skillet for 2 to 3 minutes to get rid of some of the fat. Using a slotted spoon, transfer the sausages to a plate lined with paper towels. Blot the excess fat from the slices. Stir the sausage and the zucchini into the beans, and cook for 15 minutes.

Remove the soup from the heat, and discard the bay leaf. Stir in the sherry, lemon juice, and tabasco. Serve immediately, garnished with a swirl of sour cream and a sprinkling of chopped parsley.

Makes about 6 ½ cups (Serves 4)

Sweet Corn and Crab Chowder

Creamy and rich, this chowder makes a delicious main course when served with fresh-baked bread and a salad of bitter greens. If possible, allow time for the chowder to sit uncovered for a while—from a couple of hours to overnight in the refrigerator—so the flavors can meld.

3	TABLESPOONS UNSALTED BUTTER
½	CUP FINELY CHOPPED ONION
½	CUP FINELY CHOPPED CELERY
¼	CUP ALL-PURPOSE FLOUR
4	CUPS HOMEMADE FISH STOCK OR BOTTLED CLAM JUICE
½	CUP DICED POTATO
I	CUP FRESH CORN KERNELS
I	TEASPOON CHOPPED FRESH THYME
½	TEASPOON SALT
½	TEASPOON GROUND BLACK PEPPER
I	CUP COARSELY CHOPPED WHITE CRABMEAT
I	CUP HEAVY CREAM
2	TABLESPOONS CHOPPED FRESH PARSLEY

Melt the butter in a large saucepan over medium heat, and sauté the onion and celery until softened. Stir in the flour and cook this roux for 3 minutes, stirring frequently. Gradually add the stock, whisking until you have a smooth liquid. Add the potatoes, corn, thyme, salt, and pepper. Cover and bring to a boil. Then reduce the heat and simmer for 15 minutes or until the vegetables are tender, stirring occasionally.

Stir in the crabmeat and heavy cream and heat the soup gently but thoroughly. Do not let it boil or the soup may curdle. Sprinkle with the chopped parsley, and serve immediately.

Makes about 6 cups (Serves 4)

salads

Summer Green Pea Salad

Fresh peas are the only way to go here. They're available for just a brief time in late spring and early summer, but it's definitely worth the wait—and the shelling—to enjoy their sweet flavor in this special salad.

4	CUPS SHELLED FRESH YOUNG GREEN PEAS
3	TABLESPOONS GARLIC-FLAVORED OLIVE OIL
2	TABLESPOONS BALSAMIC VINEGAR
½	CUP DICED RED BELL PEPPER
½	CUP DICED YELLOW BELL PEPPER
¼	CUP CHOPPED RED ONION
2	TABLESPOONS CHOPPED SCALLIONS
3	TABLESPOONS CHOPPED FRESH BASIL LEAVES
½	TEASPOON SALT
¼	TEASPOON GROUND BLACK PEPPER

Bring a large saucepan of salted water to a boil. Add the peas and simmer for 2 to 3 minutes or until just tender. Drain the peas and transfer them to a large bowl. Add the oil and vinegar, and toss to thoroughly coat the peas. Set them aside to cool to room temperature. When you are ready to serve the salad, gently stir in the bell peppers, red onion, scallions, basil, salt, and pepper. Serve immediately.

Makes about 5^{1}/2 cups (Serves 6)

EXOTIC FRUIT SALAD

Exotic fruits like mango, papaya, star fruit, guava, and kiwi are becoming easier to find, so experiment with different combinations. Put leftover Champagne that has gone flat to good use and mix it in with the fruit to combine with their juices and add some tang.

DRESSING

1	(11-OUNCE) CAN MANDARIN ORANGES, UNDRAINED
½	CUP FLAT CHAMPAGNE
¼	CUP SOUR CREAM
2	TABLESPOONS HONEY
1	TABLESPOON POPPY SEED

FRUIT

1	LARGE MANGO, PEELED, CUT INTO ¾-INCH CUBES (ABOUT 2 CUPS)
1	MEDIUM PAPAYA, SKIN AND SEEDS REMOVED, CUT INTO ¾-INCH CUBES (ABOUT 2 CUPS)
1	MEDIUM PINEAPPLE, SKIN, HARD EYES, AND CENTRAL CORE REMOVED, CUT INTO ¾-INCH CUBES (ABOUT 4 CUPS)
	FLAKED COCONUT OR CHOPPED NUTS, FOR GARNISH

Place the mandarin oranges, with their syrup, in a medium-size saucepan. Add the Champagne and bring to a boil. Reduce the heat and simmer until the mixture has reduced to about 1 cup. Remove from the heat and let cool.

Place the cooled mixture in a blender, and process until smooth. Stir in the sour cream, honey, and poppy seeds.

Toss the prepared fruit together in a large bowl, and pour the dressing over the fruit. Refrigerate for an hour. Decorate the fruit salad with flaked coconut or chopped nuts, and serve.

Makes about 8 cups (Serves 10 to 12)

SPICY COLESLAW

This version is spicier and more finely textured than the traditional slaw. It's the perfect accompaniment for fried fish, and the mix of red and green cabbages makes it a colorful addition to any meal.

2	CUPS FINELY SHREDDED RED CABBAGE
2	CUPS FINELY SHREDDED GREEN CABBAGE
1	CUP FINELY CHOPPED RED ONION
¾	CUP MAYONNAISE
1	TABLESPOON CIDER VINEGAR
1	TABLESPOON FRESH LEMON JUICE
1	TEASPOON DIJON MUSTARD
¼	TEASPOON SUGAR
¼	TEASPOON WORCESTERSHIRE SAUCE
⅛	TEASPOON GROUND WHITE PEPPER
⅛	TEASPOON TABASCO SAUCE

Mix the cabbages and red onion together in a large bowl. In a small bowl, whisk the remaining ingredients until smooth. Pour the dressing over the vegetables, tossing to coat them well. Chill until ready to serve, at least an hour.

Makes 6 cups (Serves 6 to 8)

Spicy Sesame Peanut Dressing

This creamy spicy dressing works as a sauce with raw or steamed vegetables or cooked rice. I also use it on green salads or as a dip.

2	TABLESPOONS PEANUT BUTTER
½	CUP TOASTED SESAME OIL
½	CUP WARM APPLE CIDER OR APPLE JUICE
I	TABLESPOON TAMARI SAUCE
I	TABLESPOON GRATED FRESH GINGER
I	TEASPOON MINCED GARLIC
½	TEASPOON GRATED LEMON ZEST
¼	TEASPOON CAYENNE PEPPER (OR TO TASTE)
2	TABLESPOONS HONEY

Whisk all the ingredients together in a small bowl. Cover and chill until needed. Shake well before using.

Makes 1 ¼ cup

Romaine Salad with Basil Vinaigrette

During my stint at waiting on tables, I learned to make a Caesar Salad. This is a lighter version of the classic Caesar. I've done away with the raw eggs because of the potential health hazard, and I've replaced the whole anchovies with paste.

I	CUP BREAD CUBES MADE FROM FRENCH BREAD
2	TABLESPOONS UNSALTED BUTTER, MELTED
¼	TEASPOON MINCED GARLIC
8	CUPS CHOPPED ROMAINE LETTUCE
¾	CUP SHAVED PARMESAN CHEESE

BASIL VINAIGRETTE

½	CUP OLIVE OIL
¼	CUP VINEGAR OR LEMON JUICE
2	TEASPOONS ANCHOVY PASTE
2	TEASPOONS MINCED GARLIC
2	TEASPOONS CHOPPED FRESH BASIL LEAVES

Preheat the oven to 375° F.

Mix the bread cubes with the melted butter, herbs, and garlic in a medium-size bowl, and then spread them out on a baking sheet. Bake for about 10 minutes, or until the cubes are golden and crisp. Let them cool.

Combine the lettuce, Parmesan, and croutons in a large serving bowl. Place all the dressing ingredients in a small bowl, and whisk until well blended. Pour the dressing over the salad, toss thoroughly, and serve immediately.

Serves 4

GRILLED SALMON SALAD WITH WILD MUSHROOMS AND ROASTED POTATOES

Not only does this dish taste great but it looks beautiful on the plate. The combination of the vivid green of the lettuce and the rosy pink of the salmon makes for a dramatic presentation. It's also hearty enough to be a main course.

DIJON DRESSING

1	TABLESPOON OLIVE OIL
¼	CUP FINELY CHOPPED SHALLOTS
1	CUP LIGHT CREAM
1	TABLESPOON DIJON MUSTARD
1½	TEASPOONS CHOPPED FRESH DILL, OR ½ TEASPOON DRIED
¼	TEASPOON SALT
¼	TEASPOON GROUND BLACK PEPPER

4	TABLESPOONS OLIVE OIL
1	POUND FRESH MUSHROOMS, SLICED
1	TABLESPOON FRESH LEMON JUICE
1	TEASPOON CHOPPED FRESH DILL, OR ½ TEASPOON DRIED
½	TEASPOON SALT
¼	TEASPOON GROUND BLACK PEPPER
4	(8-OUNCE) SALMON FILLETS
6	CUPS MIXED SALAD GREENS
2	CUPS PAPRIKA ROASTED POTATOES (SEE PAGE 156), AT ROOM TEMPERATURE

Prepare the dressing: Heat the oil in a small saucepan, and sauté the shallots over medium heat until soft. Stir in the cream, mustard, dill, salt, and pepper. Bring to a boil, then quickly lower the heat and simmer until reduced by half. Remove the pan from the heat, pour the dressing into a bowl, and set the dressing aside to cool to room temperature.

Heat 2 tablespoons of the oil in a large skillet, and sauté the mushrooms over medium heat until they are tender. Transfer them to a bowl and let cool.

Preheat the broiler or grill.

Mix together the remaining 2 tablespoons oil with the lemon juice, dill, salt, and pepper; brush this over the salmon fillets. If you are grilling, cook the fillets about 6 inches away from the heat source (if you're broiling, about 4 inches away) for 2 to 3 minutes on each side, or according to taste.

Spread the salad greens out over a large platter, and top with the cooled mushrooms. Arrange the roasted potatoes around the edge of the platter. Place the salmon fillets over the mushrooms and drizzle with the dressing. Serve immediately.

Serves 4

BLISSFUL POTATO SALAD

This is a classic southern potato salad—the one I grew up with. You can use any type of potato—Red Bliss and Yukon Gold are two of my favorites. For a lighter salad, halve the number of hard-cooked eggs and use a reduced-fat mayonnaise.

1 ½   POUNDS RED BLISS POTATOES, SCRUBBED BUT NOT PEELED

6   LARGE EGGS, HARD-COOKED AND CHOPPED

¾   CUP DICED ONION

¾   CUP DICED CELERY

¾   CUP MAYONNAISE

¼   CUP SWEET PICKLE RELISH

1   TABLESPOON YELLOW MUSTARD

½   TEASPOON SALT

½   TEASPOON GROUND BLACK PEPPER

¼   TEASPOON PAPRIKA

MIXED GREENS, FOR SERVING

OLIVES, CHOPPED GREEN BELL PEPPERS, OR SLICED CORNICHON PICKLES, FOR GARNISH

Bring a large saucepan of salted water to a boil. Add the potatoes, reduce the heat, and simmer for 15 to 20 minutes or until tender. Drain the potatoes and let them cool. Then cut them into 1-inch cubes. In a large bowl, combine the potatoes with the eggs, onion, and celery.

In a small bowl, stir together the mayonnaise, relish, mustard, salt, and pepper. Pour the dressing over the potatoes and toss gently until thoroughly combined.

Serve the potato salad on a bed of salad greens, and sprinkle the paprika over the top. Garnish with olives, chopped green peppers, or cornichon pickles, if desired.

Makes about 6 ½ cups (Serves 6 to 8)

OLIVE TAPENADE

This tapenade is very popular at the restaurant. It is a bit time-consuming to prepare—all that fine chopping—but it's worth the effort because the flavor is fantastic and it goes with just about anything—salads, cheeses, bread, meat.

¾ CUP FINELY CHOPPED PITTED KALAMATA OLIVES
½ CUP FINELY CHOPPED PITTED GREEN OLIVES
½ CUP FINELY CHOPPED RED ONION
¼ CUP FINELY CHOPPED CELERY
1 TABLESPOON FINELY CHOPPED SCALLION
¼ CUP EXTRA-VIRGIN OLIVE OIL
2 TABLESPOONS BALSAMIC VINEGAR
2 TEASPOONS MINCED GARLIC
1 TEASPOON WORCESTERSHIRE SAUCE
¼ TEASPOON TABASCO SAUCE
¼ TEASPOON SALT
¼ TEASPOON GROUND BLACK PEPPER

Combine all the ingredients in a large bowl and stir thoroughly. Cover and chill until needed, or transfer to a container with a tight fitting lid, and store in the refrigerator for up to one month.

Makes about 1 ¹/₂ cups

Note: To pit the olives, place in a single layer in a large kitchen towel on the counter. Hit the olives several times with a heavy skillet or mallet to break the flesh. The pits should then be easy to remove.

VARIATION:
QUICK BLACK OLIVE SPREAD
Place 3 cups pitted black olives, 1 large garlic clove, and ¹/₄ cup olive oil in the bowl of a food processor. Process until smooth. Transfer to a container with a tightly fitting lid, and store in the refrigerator for up to 1 month.

HONEY MUSTARD VINAIGRETTE

½ CUP EXTRA-VIRGIN OLIVE OIL
¼ CUP CIDER VINEGAR
¼ CUP HONEY
2 TABLESPOONS DIJON MUSTARD
½ TEASPOON MINCED GARLIC
1 TABLESPOON CHOPPED FRESH PARSLEY
   PINCH OF CAYENNE PEPPER

Whisk all the ingredients together in a small bowl. Cover and chill until needed.

Makes 1 cup

pasta

Fresh Pasta Dough

If you have the time (as well as willing tasters who'll bear with you through thick and thin as you perfect your technique), you'll find that making pasta by hand is a wonderfully creative and tasty process.

On the other hand a pasta machine, which rolls and cuts the dough for you, is very useful if you are in a hurry or are making a large quantity. Prepare the dough as described, and then follow the manufacturer's instructions.

2 LARGE EGGS
1½ CUPS SIFTED ALL-PURPOSE FLOUR
2 TEASPOONS OLIVE OIL
¾ TEASPOON SALT
BOILING SALTED WATER OR BROTH

Using a fork, mix the eggs, flour, olive oil, and salt together in a medium-size bowl.

Turn the dough out onto a lightly floured surface, and knead it lightly until it is smooth, about 5 minutes. Cover the dough with plastic wrap, and leave it to rest for 1 to 2 hours at room temperature. This relaxes the dough and makes it easier to roll out. (If you like, you can leave the dough in the refrigerator overnight covered with a clean kitchen towel.)

Lightly flour a work surface, and flatten the dough on it with the palm of your hand. Dust a rolling pin with flour, and roll the dough, working outward from the center, into a paper-thin sheet. Check occasionally to make sure the dough is not sticking to the surface; if it does, sprinkle a little more flour on the surface. Cut the dough into $^1/_4$-inch-thick strips or the shape of your choice, or use it to make filled pasta as in Lobster Ravioli (see page 125).

Cook in water or broth for 2 to 3 minutes. Drain. Serve immediately.

Serves 4 as an appetizer, 2 as a main course

LOBSTER RAVIOLI WITH TOMATO CREAM SAUCE

This ravioli—filled with lobster and lightly tossed with a sublime cream sauce—is the height of elegance.

FILLING

1½	CUPS CHOPPED COOKED LOBSTER MEAT
⅓	CUP RICOTTA CHEESE
1	TABLESPOON GRATED PARMESAN CHEESE
1	TABLESPOON MINCED SCALLIONS
1	TEASPOON MINCED FRESH PARSLEY
½	TEASPOON CHOPPED FRESH DILL
½	TEASPOON WORCESTERSHIRE SAUCE
⅛	TEASPOON TABASCO SAUCE
½	TEASPOON SALT
2	RECIPES FRESH PASTA DOUGH (SEE PAGE 123), ROLLED OUT INTO 2 LARGE PAPER-THIN RECTANGLES
2	CUPS ROASTED PLUM TOMATO SAUCE (SEE PAGE 40)
1	CUP HEAVY CREAM
2	TEASPOONS CHOPPED FRESH TARRAGON CHOPPED COOKED LOBSTER OR DICED FRESH PLUM TOMATO, FOR GARNISH CHOPPED FRESH TARRAGON, FOR GARNISH

Place all the filling ingredients in a large bowl, and stir to combine. Lay one pasta sheet on a lightly floured surface, and place heaping teaspoons of the filling on the pasta at 1½-inch intervals, in lines 1½ inches apart, until you have reached the center of the sheet. Brush the edges of the dough with water. Fold the uncovered side of the dough over, so that the edges meet. Pinch to seal the edges. Using a fluted pastry wheel, cut down the length of the dough between the mounds of filling. Then cut each strip into individual ravioli parcels. Repeat with the second rectangle of pasta dough and the remaining filling. Arrange the ravioli in a single layer on a floured dish towel, and let them dry for about 1 hour, turning them over after 30 minutes.

Bring a large pot of salted water to a boil. Add the ravioli, and cook for 10 to 12 minutes or until the pasta is just tender.

Meanwhile, heat the tomato sauce until it is simmering. Stir in the cream and tarragon, and gently bring the sauce back to the simmering point. Remove the pan from the heat. Drain the ravioli carefully and serve immediately with the tomato cream sauce, garnished with pieces of lobster or tomato and chopped tarragon.

Serves 4 to 6 (depending on how thin the pasta is rolled)

Pasta Primavera

This is a simple yet elegant version of a pasta primavera (which means "springtime")—a dish that should be made with only the freshest vegetables and herbs available, either from your garden or from the produce market. The possible variations are endless. Be sure to serve this pasta in bowls, because you'll want to spoon up the delicious broth.

I	POUND PASTA OF YOUR CHOICE
¼	CUP EXTRA-VIRGIN OLIVE OIL
2	TEASPOONS MINCED GARLIC
6	CUPS MIXED SEASONAL VEGETABLES (SUCH AS CHOPPED CARROTS, ASPARAGUS TIPS, FRESH PEAS, CORN KERNELS)
I ½	CUPS HOMEMADE CHICKEN STOCK OR CANNED BROTH
¼	CUP CHOPPED FRESH BASIL LEAVES
2	TABLESPOONS CHOPPED FRESH PARSLEY
½	TEASPOON SALT
¼	TEASPOON GROUND BLACK PEPPER FRESHLY GRATED PARMESAN CHEESE (OPTIONAL)

Bring a large pot of salted water to a boil. Add the pasta and cook according to the package directions until it is just tender.

Meanwhile, heat the oil in a large skillet. Add the garlic and vegetables, and sauté for 4 to 5 minutes over medium heat, or until just tender. Add the chicken stock, basil, parsley, salt, and pepper, and bring to a boil over high heat. Remove the skillet from the heat and keep warm.

Drain the pasta thoroughly and transfer it to a warmed serving bowl. Toss it with the vegetable sauce and serve immediately, sprinkled with freshly grated Parmesan, if desired.

Serves 4

Old-Fashioned Baked Macaroni and Cheese

This was pasta to me before my visits to Italy and before pasta became fashionable. Dan and Dana wouldn't let me leave this favorite family recipe out of the book. The addition of vegetables or ground meat creates a hearty variation.

2	CUPS ELBOW MACARONI
2	LARGE EGGS
2	CUPS EVAPORATED MILK
2	TABLESPOONS UNSALTED BUTTER, MELTED
I	TEASPOON WORCESTERSHIRE SAUCE
¼	TEASPOON SALT
⅛	TEASPOON CAYENNE PEPPER
2	CUPS GRATED CHEDDAR CHEESE

Preheat the oven to 350° F.

Bring a large pot of salted water to a boil. Add the macaroni and cook for 10 to 12 minutes or until it is just tender.

Meanwhile beat together the eggs, evaporated milk, melted butter, Worcestershire, salt, and cayenne pepper in a medium-size bowl.

Drain the macaroni thoroughly. Layer the macaroni and cheddar in a I ½-quart ovenproof dish, ending with a layer of cheese. Pour the egg mixture over, and bake for 35 to 40 minutes, until golden brown and bubbling. Serve immediately.

Serves 4

TRICOLOR PASTA SALAD

You can't beat this salad for its versatility—it accommodates all sorts of additions and substitutions. The addition of fresh cooked tuna makes for a hearty dish, and peas, carrots, and corn will add texture and color. It can be eaten warm or at room temperature, and I've even been known to eat it straight out of the fridge!

DRESSING

⅓   CUP EXTRA-VIRGIN OLIVE OIL

¼   CUP BALSAMIC VINEGAR

¼   CUP GRATED PARMESAN CHEESE

2   TEASPOONS MINCED GARLIC

1   TABLESPOON WORCESTERSHIRE SAUCE

1   TABLESPOON SUGAR

¼   TEASPOON TABASCO SAUCE

1   (7-OUNCE) JAR SUN-DRIED TOMATOES IN OLIVE OIL, DRAINED (RESERVE THE OIL) AND CHOPPED

1   POUND TRICOLOR FUSILLI, OR OTHER SHORT PASTA

2   CUPS CHOPPED MIXED RED, YELLOW, AND GREEN BELL PEPPERS

¼   CUP CHOPPED FRESH BASIL

1½   CUPS SLIVERED RED ONIONS

Bring a large pot of salted water to a boil.

While the water is heating, combine the dressing ingredients in a medium-size bowl. Add the oil from the sun-dried tomatoes, and whisk thoroughly.

Add the pasta to the boiling water and cook according to the package directions, until it is just tender. Drain the pasta thoroughly, rinse it under warm water, and drain it again. In a large serving bowl, toss the pasta with the bell peppers, sun-dried tomatoes, basil, and three-quarters of the red onion.

Pour the dressing over the salad and toss well. Garnish with the remaining slivers of red onion, and serve immediately.

Serves 4 to 6

Spinach Fettuccine with Chicken in a Spicy Tomato Sauce

Here's a dish I trick people with. They think they're getting something very decadent because of the rich and spicy cream sauce—but they're also getting their spinach and loving it!

2	TABLESPOONS VIRGIN OLIVE OIL
12	OUNCES BONELESS SKINLESS CHICKEN BREASTS, CUT INTO JULIENNE STRIPS (ABOUT 1½ CUPS)
2	TEASPOONS MINCED GARLIC
1½	CUPS SMALL BROCCOLI FLORETS
1	CUP JULIENNED LEEKS
1	CUP JULIENNED MIXED RED, YELLOW, AND GREEN BELL PEPPERS
½	CUP JULIENNED SUN-DRIED TOMATOES
1	CUP CANNED PLUM TOMATOES, CHOPPED, WITH THEIR JUICE
½	TEASPOON DRIED RED PEPPER FLAKES
½	TEASPOON SALT
1	CUP HEAVY CREAM
1	POUND SPINACH FETTUCCINE FRESHLY GRATED PARMESAN CHEESE (OPTIONAL)

Bring a large pot of salted water to a boil.

While the water is heating, heat the oil in a large skillet over medium heat. Add the chicken and garlic, and sauté for 3 to 4 minutes, tossing constantly. Then add the broccoli, leeks, and bell peppers, and sauté for 5 minutes or until the vegetables are just tender. Stir in the sun-dried tomatoes, plum tomatoes, red pepper flakes, and salt. Bring to a boil; then reduce the heat, cover, and simmer for 5 minutes.

Stir in the heavy cream, and reheat the sauce gently.

Meanwhile, cook the fettuccine in the boiling water according to the package directions, until it is just tender. Drain it thoroughly, and toss with the sauce. Serve immediately, sprinkled with freshly grated Parmesan if desired.

Serves 4

Bow-Tie Pasta with Smoked Salmon and Dill

I always have a supply of spaghetti, vermicelli, or linguine on hand. For a treat I like to use bowl-ties (farfalle), which make me think of tuxes and give this dish a formal air. I even served it at my wedding dinner!

1	POUND BOW-TIE PASTA
2	CUPS HEAVY CREAM
2	CUPS DICED SMOKED SALMON
1	CUP CHOPPED SEEDED FRESH PLUM TOMATOES
1	TABLESPOON CHOPPED FRESH DILL
¼	TEASPOON GROUND BLACK PEPPER
1	CUP CHOPPED COOKED ASPARAGUS (OPTIONAL)

Bring a large pot of salted water to a boil. Add the pasta, and cook according to the package directions until it is just tender.

Meanwhile, bring the heavy cream to a gentle boil in a skillet over low heat. Stir in the smoked salmon, plum tomatoes, dill, pepper, and the asparagus if you are using it. Cook for 30 seconds. Then remove the skillet from the heat.

Drain the pasta thoroughly and transfer it to a warmed serving bowl. Toss it with the sauce, and serve immediately.

Serves 4

RIGATONI WITH GROUND VEAL AND SAGE

I fell in love with a version of this dish when I experienced fresh sage for the first time. It has a thrilling effect when combined with veal, but you can also use ground duck, turkey, or chicken.

¼	CUP OLIVE OIL
2	TEASPOONS MINCED GARLIC
1½	POUNDS GROUND VEAL
1	CUP CHOPPED GREEN BELL PEPPERS
½	CUP CHOPPED SCALLIONS
1	CUP HOMEMADE VEAL OR CHICKEN STOCK, OR CANNED BROTH
2	CUPS SLICED MUSHROOMS
¼	CUP FINELY CHOPPED FRESH SAGE LEAVES
2	BAY LEAVES
1½	TEASPOONS SALT
½	TEASPOON GROUND BLACK PEPPER
1	POUND RIGATONI

Bring a large pot of salted water to a boil.

While the water is heating, heat the oil in a large skillet. Add the garlic and ground veal and cook over medium heat, stirring with a wooden spoon to break up any lumps, for 10 minutes or until the veal begins to lose its pink color. Add the bell peppers and scallions, and sauté for 2 minutes. Then stir in the stock, mushrooms, sage, bay leaves, salt, and pepper. Bring to a boil, cover, and simmer for about 15 minutes.

Meanwhile, add the rigatoni to the boiling water and cook according to the package directions until it is just tender. Drain thoroughly and transfer to a warmed serving bowl.

Remove the skillet from the heat and discard the bay leaves. Pour the sauce over the cooked pasta and toss together. Serve immediately.

Serves 4

SPAGHETTI WITH CLAM SAUCE

The presentation of this dish always elicits oohs and aahs from my guests. At the restaurant and at home, I serve the pasta covered with a mound of chopped clams and ringed with small clams still in their steam-opened shells.

1	POUND SPAGHETTI
6	TABLESPOONS OLIVE OIL
½	CUP CHOPPED ONION
2	TEASPOONS MINCED GARLIC
½	CUP DRY WHITE WINE
½	CUP BOTTLED CLAM JUICE
1	CUP MINCED FRESH CLAMS
½	CUP DICED SEEDED TOMATO
½	TEASPOON CHOPPED FRESH OREGANO
½	TEASPOON SALT
¼	TEASPOON GROUND BLACK PEPPER
2	POUNDS BABY CLAMS, STEAMED UNTIL THE SHELLS BEGIN TO OPEN

Bring a large pot of salted water to a boil. Add the spaghetti and cook for 8 to 10 minutes or until just tender.

Meanwhile, heat the oil in a large skillet. Add the onion and garlic, and cook over medium heat until softened. Then add the white wine, clam juice, minced clams, tomato, oregano, salt, and pepper. Bring to a boil over medium heat and cook for 5 minutes.

Drain the spaghetti thoroughly, mound it in a large serving bowl, and pour the clam sauce over it. Top with the whole steamed clams and serve.

Serves 4

seafood

GRILLED SHRIMP WITH MANGO GLACÉ AND PLANTAINS

The mango is what gives this dish its exotic flavor. The fruit blends beautifully with the sweet plantains and will satisfy the fiercest cravings for Caribbean cuisine.

2   POUNDS LARGE SHRIMP (ABOUT 20),
    PEELED AND DEVEINED, TAILS LEFT ON

MARINADE

2   TABLESPOONS SESAME OIL
1   TABLESPOON HOISIN SAUCE
1   TABLESPOON OYSTER SAUCE
2   TEASPOONS HONEY
¼   CUP MINCED SCALLIONS
1   TABLESPOON GRATED FRESH GINGER
1   TEASPOON MINCED GARLIC
⅛   TEASPOON SALT
⅛   TEASPOON GROUND BLACK PEPPER
    FEW DROPS OF TABASCO SAUCE

MANGO GLACÉ

2   LARGE EGG YOLKS
1   TEASPOON FRESH LEMON JUICE
2   DROPS OF WORCESTERSHIRE SAUCE
1   DROP OF TABASCO SAUCE
¼   TEASPOON SALT
¼   TEASPOON GROUND BLACK PEPPER
8   TABLESPOONS UNSALTED BUTTER
½   CUP HEAVY CREAM, WHIPPED UNTIL STIFF
½   CUP FRESH OR FROZEN (THAWED)
    MANGO PURÉE

2   TABLESPOONS VEGETABLE OIL
2   MEDIUM-SIZE PLANTAINS, PEELED,
    EACH CUT INTO 10 SLICES
    LIME SLICES, FOR GARNISH
    CHOPPED FRESH PARSLEY, FOR GARNISH

Rinse the shrimp and pat them dry with paper towels. Mix the marinade ingredients together in a small bowl. Place the shrimp in a shallow dish or plastic container, and pour the marinade over them. Cover and marinate for 1 to 2 hours in the refrigerator, turning once.

Prepare a grill.

Combine the egg yolks, lemon juice, Worcestershire, Tabasco, salt, and pepper in the top of a double boiler over low heat, and whisk until fluffy. Then whisk in the butter, a tablespoon at a time, making sure each tablespoon is incorporated before adding the next. Fold in the whipped cream and mango purée, and gently heat through, stirring frequently. Keep warm over very low heat.

Heat the oil in a large skillet, and cook the plantain slices over medium heat until golden and tender, about 2 to 3 minutes per side. Using a slotted spatula, transfer the plantains to a dish and keep warm.

Remove the shrimp from the marinade, and grill them 4 to 6 inches away from the heat source for 2 minutes on each side, or until pink and just cooked through. Spoon one fourth of the Mango Glacé onto each serving plate, and place each plate under the broiler for 1 minute. Arrange the shrimp and plantains, alternating, around the edge. Serve immediately, garnished with lime slices and chopped parsley.

Serves 4

Fillets of Sole with Herbal Beurre Blanc

Despite its formal name, this classic dish is one of the easiest to prepare and remains the favorite of many a chef, who can always rely on the popularity of this tried-and-true favorite.

BEURRE BLANC

¼	CUP FINELY CHOPPED SHALLOTS
¼	CUP DRY WHITE WINE
¼	CUP WHITE WINE VINEGAR
¼	CUP HEAVY CREAM
1	CUP UNSALTED BUTTER
1	TEASPOON FINELY CHOPPED FRESH TARRAGON
1	TEASPOON FINELY CHOPPED FRESH BASIL
½	TEASPOON SALT
¼	TEASPOON GROUND WHITE PEPPER

4	(8-OUNCE) SOLE FILLETS
¼	CUP ALL-PURPOSE FLOUR
¼	TEASPOON SALT
⅛	TEASPOON GROUND BLACK PEPPER
2	TABLESPOONS UNSALTED BUTTER
	FRESH PARSLEY SPRIGS, FOR GARNISH

Bring the shallots, wine, and vinegar to a boil in a medium-size saucepan. Reduce the heat and gently simmer until the liquid has reduced to 2 tablespoons. Then stir in the cream. Whisk in the butter, 1 tablespoon at a time, until all the butter has been incorporated. Stir in the tarragon, basil, salt, and white pepper. Keep warm over very low heat while you cook the fish.

Rinse the fillets and pat them dry with paper towels. Sift the flour, salt, and pepper together onto a large plate. Coat each fillet with the flour mixture, shaking off any excess. Heat the butter in a large skillet, and cook the fish for about 3 minutes on each side, until the fillets are golden and the fish flakes easily when tested with a fork. Using a slotted spatula, transfer the fillets to a serving platter. Serve immediately with the beurre blanc, garnished with parsley sprigs, if desired.

Serves 4

Seared Tuna with Coconut Curry Sauce

Coconut and curry are a classic Caribbean combination, and they come together here in a knockout blend that transforms the tuna. For a thoroughly traditional meal, serve the tuna with Banana Hash (page 93) and Pigeon Peas and Rice (page 155).

COCONUT CURRY SAUCE

1	CUP HOMEMADE FISH STOCK OR BOTTLED CLAM JUICE
1	CUP CANNED COCONUT MILK
½	CUP CANNED CREAM OF COCONUT
2	GARLIC CLOVES, CRUSHED
2	TABLESPOONS CHOPPED FRESH GINGER
½	CUP MINCED SCALLIONS
2	TABLESPOONS CHOPPED LEMON GRASS (OPTIONAL)
2	TABLESPOONS CURRY POWDER
2	TABLESPOONS LIGHT SOY SAUCE
½	TEASPOON DRIED RED PEPPER FLAKES

4	(8-OUNCE) TUNA STEAKS
½	TEASPOON SALT
1	TEASPOON COARSELY GROUND BLACK PEPPER
2	TABLESPOONS OLIVE OIL

Combine all the sauce ingredients in a medium-size saucepan and bring to a boil over medium heat. Reduce the heat and simmer for 15 minutes, stirring occasionally. Remove the pan from the heat and strain the sauce through a sieve, pressing as much of the sauce through as possible. Return the sauce to a clean saucepan and keep it warm.

Rinse the tuna steaks and pat them dry with paper towels. Rub them with the salt and coarse pepper. Heat the oil in a large skillet over medium-high heat, and sear the steaks for 3 to 4 minutes on each side (or to taste). Spoon a pool of Coconut Curry Sauce onto each plate, and set the tuna on top of the sauce. Serve immediately.

Serves 4

Flash-Roasted Salmon with Swiss Chard and Citrus Vinaigrette

The most difficult part of putting together this dish is squeezing the fruit for the citrus juice!

4   (8-OUNCE) SALMON FILLETS

2   TABLESPOONS UNSALTED BUTTER, SOFTENED

¼   CUP MINCED SHALLOTS

¼   TEASPOON SALT

¼   TEASPOON GROUND BLACK PEPPER

½   CUP DRY WHITE WINE

CITRUS VINAIGRETTE

½   CUP OLIVE OIL

1   TABLESPOON FRESH ORANGE JUICE

1   TABLESPOON FRESH LEMON JUICE

1   TABLESPOON FRESH LIME JUICE

1   TEASPOON FINELY CHOPPED FRESH TARRAGON

¼   TEASPOON SALT

¼   TEASPOON GROUND BLACK PEPPER

2   CUPS SWISS CHARD LEAVES, BLANCHED FOR 30 SECONDS IN BOILING WATER

ORANGE, LEMON, AND LIME ZEST, CUT IN JULIENNE STRIPS, FOR GARNISH

Preheat the oven to 425° F. Rinse the salmon fillets and pat them dry with paper towels.

Arrange the salmon in a roasting pan, and spread ¹/₂ tablespoon of the butter over each fillet. Sprinkle with the shallots, salt, and pepper. Pour the wine over the fish, and roast for 10 minutes or to taste. Transfer the fillets to a serving platter and keep warm.

Whisk the vinaigrette ingredients together in a small bowl. Top the salmon fillets with the blanched Swiss chard, and pour the vinaigrette over all. Serve immediately, sprinkled with the lemon, lime, and orange zest, if desired.

Serves 4

GRILLED SEAFOOD BROCHETTES

Great on the outdoor grill, these also broil well in the oven. Keep an eye on them, though, because no matter where you cook them, they require just a few minutes—otherwise they'll dry out.

12	LARGE SHRIMP (ABOUT 1 POUND), PEELED AND DEVEINED
16	SEA SCALLOPS (ABOUT 8 OUNCES)
1	POUND FRESH TUNA, CUT INTO 16 PIECES
1	LARGE GREEN BELL PEPPER, CUT INTO 16 PIECES
3	SMALL ONIONS, QUARTERED
8	CHERRY TOMATOES

MARINADE

1	CUP OLIVE OIL
½	CUP FRESH LEMON JUICE
2	TEASPOONS MINCED GARLIC
2	TEASPOONS GROUND GINGER
½	TEASPOON SALT
½	TEASPOON GROUND BLACK PEPPER

LEMON WEDGES, FOR GARNISH

Rinse the seafood and pat it dry with paper towels. Thread the seafood, bell pepper, onions, and cherry tomatoes onto four long skewers. Lay them in a large shallow dish or plastic container.

Mix all the marinade ingredients together in a medium-size bowl, and pour over the brochettes. Cover and marinate for 1 to 2 hours in the refrigerator, turning once.

Prepare a grill.

Remove the brochettes from the marinade, and grill them, 4 to 6 inches away from the heat source, for about 3 minutes on each side or until the seafood is just cooked. Serve immediately, garnished with lemon wedges.

Serves 4

Variation: To turn this recipe into a warm seafood salad, follow the instructions below.

GRILLED SEAFOOD SALAD

1	RECIPE GRILLED SEAFOOD BROCHETTES, OMITTING THE VEGETABLES
8	CUPS MIXED SALAD GREENS

LIME VINAIGRETTE

6	TABLESPOONS OLIVE OIL
1	TABLESPOON BALSAMIC VINEGAR
1	TABLESPOON FRESH LIME JUICE
¼	TEASPOON SALT

Prepare, marinate, and cook the seafood as described above, omitting the vegetables. Spread the salad greens out over a large platter, and lay the brochettes on the top.

Whisk the ingredients for the Lime Vinaigrette together in a small bowl, and pour the dressing over the brochettes and greens. Serve warm.

Serves 4

Sea Bass with Orange-Ginger Sauce

I created this recipe one day when I was trying to use whatever I had on hand. There's usually a supply of fresh ginger in my refrigerator and I always have oranges to squeeze for juice, and so—voilà!—this sauce was born. The rum adds a nice note of sass.

4   (8-ounce) sea bass fillets

Orange-Ginger Sauce

¼   cup fresh orange juice

2   tablespoons grated fresh ginger

2   teaspoons orange marmalade

3   tablespoons olive oil

3   tablespoons unsalted butter

¼   cup homemade fish stock or bottled clam juice

3   tablespoons dark rum

¼   cup heavy cream

½   teaspoon salt

¼   teaspoon ground black pepper

chopped fresh chives, for garnish

Rinse the sea bass fillets and pat them dry with paper towels. Place the fillets in a shallow dish or plastic container. In a small bowl, stir together the orange juice, ginger, marmalade, and 2 tablespoons of the olive oil. Pour this over the fish, cover the dish, and marinate for 20 minutes, turning once.

Remove the fish from the marinade and blot the fillets dry on paper towels (reserve the marinade). Heat the remaining 1 tablespoon olive oil with the butter in a large skillet. Cook the fillets for about 3 minutes on each side, or until they are golden brown and the fish flakes easily when tested with a fork. Using a slotted spatula, transfer the fish to a serving platter and keep warm.

Discard all but 1 tablespoon of the residual fat in the skillet. Stir in the stock, rum, and reserved marinade. Bring to a gentle boil, scraping up the cooked juices on the bottom of the pan. Then stir in the cream, salt, and pepper, and reheat gently. Pour the sauce over the fish, garnish with chopped chives, and serve immediately.

Serves 4

GROUPER WITH CHAMPAGNE SAFFRON CREAM

Grouper is taken to a new height of style and taste with this light and elegant cream sauce. The distinct flavor and golden color of the saffron will work its magic on your most discerning guest.

4   (8-OUNCE) GROUPER FILLETS
½   TEASPOON SALT
¼   TEASPOON GROUND BLACK PEPPER

CHAMPAGNE SAFFRON CREAM

　　 PINCH OF SAFFRON THREADS
1   TABLESPOON MILK, WARMED
1½   CUPS CHAMPAGNE
½   CUP CHOPPED SHALLOTS
2   SPRIGS FRESH THYME
2   GARLIC CLOVES
1   CUP HEAVY CREAM
3   TABLESPOONS UNSALTED BUTTER
　　 SALT
　　 GROUND BLACK PEPPER

½   CUP UNSALTED BUTTER

　　 FRESH THYME SPRIGS, FOR GARNISH

Rinse the grouper fillets and pat them dry with paper towels. Sprinkle them with the salt and pepper, cover, and set aside. Sprinkle the saffron over the warmed milk in a small teacup, and leave to soak for 10 minutes.

Combine the Champagne, shallots, thyme, garlic cloves, and half the saffron mixture in a medium-size saucepan. Bring to a boil, reduce the heat, and simmer until the liquid has reduced to about $^1/_2$ cup. Strain the liquid into a clean saucepan. Stir in the cream and then whisk in the 3 tablespoons butter, a tablespoon at a time, until all the butter has been incorporated. Add the remaining saffron mixture, and the salt and pepper. Keep warm over very low heat while you cook the fish.

Heat the $^1/_2$ cup butter in a large skillet. Cook the fillets for about 3 minutes on each side, or until the flesh flakes easily when tested with a fork. Using a slotted spatula, transfer the fillets to a serving platter. Serve immediately with the saffron sauce, garnished with fresh thyme sprigs if desired.

Serves 4

SOFT-SHELL CRABS WITH LEMON CAPER SAUCE

I'm always excited when it's soft-shell crab season because they are so tasty and so simple to prepare. If you've never had these delectable creatures, this dish is a great introduction.

1	CUP ALL-PURPOSE FLOUR
1	TEASPOON SALT
½	TEASPOON GROUND BLACK PEPPER
½	TEASPOON OLD BAY SEASONING (OPTIONAL)
4	LARGE (OR 8 SMALL) SOFT-SHELL CRABS, CLEANED
½	CUP UNSALTED BUTTER
½	CUP DRY WHITE WINE
¼	CUP FRESH LEMON JUICE
¼	CUP WATER
¼	CUP CAPERS, DRAINED
	LEMON WEDGES, FOR GARNISH
	CHOPPED FRESH PARSLEY, FOR GARNISH

In a shallow dish, mix together the flour, salt, pepper, and Old Bay Seasoning. Dip the crabs into the flour mixture to thoroughly coat them. Shake off any excess flour.

Melt half the butter in a large skillet and cook two of the crabs over medium-high heat for 2 to 3 minutes on each side, or until cooked through. Transfer them to a serving platter and keep warm. Repeat with the remaining butter and crabs.

Add the remaining ingredients to the skillet and bring to a boil, scraping up all the cooked juices from the bottom. Pour the sauce over the crabs and serve immediately, garnished with lemon wedges and chopped parsley, if desired.

Serves 4

meat and poultry

CORNBREAD CHICKEN POT PIE

My mother taught me how to make creamed chicken and dumplings, but I discovered on my own that cornbread batter holds up better than dumplings—especially when I make large amounts of this creamed chicken.

1   (3½-POUND) CHICKEN
5   CUPS WATER
1   ONION
2   RIBS CELERY, CHOPPED
2   BAY LEAVES
1   SPRIG FRESH THYME
6   PEPPERCORNS

SAUCE

2   TABLESPOONS UNSALTED BUTTER
½   CUP CHOPPED ONIONS
½   CUP CHOPPED CELERY
2   CUPS CHICKEN STOCK OR CANNED BROTH
1   CUP MILK
6   TABLESPOONS ALL-PURPOSE FLOUR
1   (10-OUNCE) PACKAGE FROZEN MIXED
    VEGETABLES, THAWED AND DRAINED
1   TABLESPOON CHOPPED FRESH PARSLEY
1   TEASPOON SALT
¼   TEASPOON GROUND BLACK PEPPER

CORNBREAD

1¼ CUPS YELLOW CORNMEAL
1   CUP ALL-PURPOSE FLOUR
2½ TEASPOONS BAKING POWDER
1   TEASPOON SUGAR
1   TEASPOON SALT
¼   TEASPOON CHILI POWDER
1   CUP MILK
2   LARGE EGGS
¼   CUP VEGETABLE OIL OR MELTED BUTTER

Rinse the chicken with cold water, and pat it dry with paper towels. Place it in a large pot and add the water, onion, celery, bay leaves, thyme, and peppercorns. Bring to a boil, reduce the heat, cover, and simmer for 1 to 1 ¼ hours or until the chicken is cooked through. Transfer the chicken to a large plate and let it cool slightly. Then remove all the meat from the carcass, discarding the skin and bones. Set the meat aside. Strain the stock and reserve 2 cups; place on low heat to keep it hot.

Next, prepare the sauce: Melt the butter in a large saucepan. Over medium high heat add chopped onions and celery and sauté until softened. Stir in the stock and the milk. In a separate bowl mix flour with ½ cup water and gradually whisk into liquid in saucepan. Cook over medium heat for 4 to 5 minutes, until the sauce has thickened. Stir in the drained vegetables, parsley, salt, pepper, and chicken meat. Pour into a 3-quart baking dish and set aside.

Preheat the oven to 375° F.

Stir together the cornmeal, flour, baking powder, sugar, salt, and chili powder in a large bowl. In a medium bowl, whisk the milk, eggs, and oil together. Stir the milk mixture into the dry ingredients until just combined. Spoon the batter over the chicken mixture. Bake for 50 minutes to 1 hour, or until the cornbread is well risen and a toothpick inserted in the center of it comes out clean. Let stand 10 minutes before serving.

Serves 6

CHITTERLINGS

Chitlins, or chitterlings, as they are formally called, were considered a delicacy when I was growing up. Today they're a rarity, for there aren't too many people left who are familiar with the time-consuming and labor-intensive art of chitlin (pig intestine) preparation. Chitterlings come frozen and require thorough cleaning before cooking. Overnight refrigeration helps remove some of the odor.

10	POUNDS CHITTERLINGS
¼	CUP DISTILLED WHITE VINEGAR
1	CUP CUBED POTATO
½	CUP COARSELY CHOPPED ONION
3	GARLIC CLOVES
3	BAY LEAVES
1	TEASPOON SALT (OR TO TASTE)
1	TEASPOON DRIED RED PEPPER FLAKES
½	TEASPOON GROUND BLACK PEPPER
1	TEASPOON CHOPPED FRESH THYME LEAVES, OR ½ TEASPOON DRIED

Place the chitterlings in a large pot and add cold water to cover the vinegar and soak for 1 hour at room temperature. Drain the chitterlings and remove the dirt and excess fat. Cover them with clean cold water, and soak for up to 24 hours in the refrigerator. Drain, and rinse once more with cold water.

Place the chitterlings in a large pot and bring to a boil. Remove approximately 4 cups of the juices as they accumulate, and stir in the remaining ingredients. Bring to a boil, reduce the heat, cover, and simmer for 3½ to 4 hours or until tender. Drain, and serve immediately.

Makes about 4 cups (Serves 6)

MOM'S FRIED CHICKEN

I can't begin to guess how much fried chicken I've cooked in my lifetime! Because it was a staple in our home during my childhood, it was a rite of passage for each girl child to learn to fry chicken like the womenfolk.

1	(3-POUND) FRYER CHICKEN, CUT INTO SERVING PIECES
1	TEASPOON SALT
1	TEASPOON GROUND BLACK PEPPER
1	TEASPOON GARLIC POWDER (OPTIONAL)
1	TEASPOON POULTRY SEASONING (OPTIONAL)
2	CUPS VEGETABLE OIL
1½	CUPS ALL-PURPOSE FLOUR

Rinse the chicken pieces with cold water and pat them dry with paper towels. Sprinkle the chicken with the salt and pepper, and with the garlic powder and poultry seasoning if you are using them. Cover and set aside for 15 minutes, or refrigerate for up to 12 hours.

Pour the oil into a deep skillet and heat it to 350° F.

Meanwhile, place the flour in a large self-sealing food storage bag. Add the chicken pieces, a few at a time, and shake to thoroughly coat them. Dust off any excess flour.

Fry the chicken, a few pieces at a time, in the hot oil for 25 to 30 minutes, turning once, until they are golden brown and cooked through. Drain on paper towels, and serve warm or at room temperature.

Serves 4

DUCK SAUSAGE

When I lived in Austria and Germany I enjoyed the many types of sausages there. In this recipe I use duck, which isn't as fatty as pork or beef and which I think is a sophisticated alternative to them.

2	POUNDS DUCK BREAST MEAT
I	CUP UNSEASONED DRIED BREAD CRUMBS
I	CUP FINELY CHOPPED ONION
4	TEASPOONS MINCED GARLIC
I	TEASPOON SALT
I ½	TEASPOONS CRUSHED FENNEL SEED
I	TEASPOON DRIED THYME
I	TEASPOON DRIED OREGANO
I	TEASPOON DRIED PARSLEY
I	TEASPOON PAPRIKA
I	TEASPOON CAYENNE PEPPER
I	TEASPOON GROUND BLACK PEPPER
⅛	TEASPOON TABASCO SAUCE
	FRESH SALTED HOG SAUSAGE CASINGS, THOROUGHLY CLEANED (OPTIONAL)

Grind the duck meat coarsely in a meat grinder or food processor, or chop it by hand. (If you use a food processor, grind the meat by "pulsing" to prevent overprocessing.) Transfer the meat to a large bowl, add the remaining ingredients (except the casings), and mix very thoroughly.

Either form the meat into patties or stuff it into the hog casings (using a commercial sausage stuffer or the stuffing attachment on an electric meat grinder; follow the manufacturer's directions).

Cook the sausages on a grill or under the broiler for 10 to 15 minutes, turning them frequently, until they are well browned and cooked through. If making patties, cook in a nonstick frying pan or broil 2 to 3 minutes per side. These sausages freeze well and reheat beautifully.

Makes about 14 (4-inch) sausages or (¹/₂-inch thick) patties

SMOTHERED PORK CHOPS

This dish is an updated version of a recipe I got from my mother, who was very hard to please. On a visit to New York she tried *my* smothered pork chops and raved about them. If these passed her taste test, they must be good!

¼	CUP ALL-PURPOSE FLOUR
1	TEASPOON SALT
½	TEASPOON GROUND BLACK PEPPER
8	(½-INCH-THICK) PORK CHOPS (4 TO 6 OUNCES EACH), TRIMMED OF FAT
2	TABLESPOONS OLIVE OIL
1	TABLESPOON UNSALTED BUTTER
1	CUP THINLY SLICED ONIONS
1	CUP HOMEMADE CHICKEN STOCK OR CANNED BROTH
½	CUP HEAVY CREAM

Stir the flour, salt, and pepper together in a small cup and spread the mixture out on a large plate. Dip the pork chops into the flour mixture on both sides. Shake off any excess.

Heat the oil in a large skillet, and cook the chops over medium-high heat until well done. Transfer them to a serving platter and keep warm. Add the butter to the same skillet and heat it over medium-high heat. Stir in the onions and sauté until they are soft and dark golden brown. Then stir in the chicken stock and bring to a boil. Gradually add the cream and gently reheat, stirring constantly, for 2 to 3 minutes or until the sauce has thickened. Pour the sauce over the pork chops and serve immediately.

Serves 4

VEAL CHOPS WITH SAGE

Our garden always had plenty of vegetables but never herbs, so when I was introduced to fresh herbs it opened up a new world. This chop is enhanced by the fresh sage—pounded into the meat with a mallet—which infuses the veal and makes it very fragrant and wonderfully flavorful.

4	(8-OUNCE) VEAL CHOPS
2	TEASPOONS CHOPPED FRESH SAGE
½	TEASPOON SALT
¼	TEASPOON GROUND BLACK PEPPER
⅓	CUP ALL-PURPOSE FLOUR
2	TABLESPOONS OLIVE OIL
1	CUP HOMEMADE VEAL OR BEEF STOCK, OR CANNED BROTH
1	CUP DRY WHITE WINE
1	TEASPOON SLIVERED FRESH SAGE LEAVES

Place the veal chops on a cutting board, and sprinkle them with the chopped sage, salt, and pepper. Pound the chops with a mallet until they are about ½-inch-thick and the herbs are worked into the flesh. Spread the flour out on a plate and liberally coat the chops on each side.

Heat the oil in a large skillet, and cook the chops over medium-high heat according to taste. Transfer them to a serving platter and keep warm. Stir the stock, wine, and sage slivers into the skillet and bring to a boil, scraping up all the cooked juices from the bottom. Reduce the heat and simmer for 2 to 3 minutes, until the sauce has thickened. Pour the sauce over the chops and serve immediately.

Serves 4

meat and poultry 149

Marinated Filet Mignon with Mushrooms

If you start out with a great cut of meat and marinate it, the meat can stand alone—there's no need for a sauce. For a more festive dinner, though, the addition of this mushroom and shallot sauce makes for a spectacular dish. I like to use a combination of different types of mushrooms.

4 (8-OUNCE) FILETS MIGNONS

MARINADE

¼ CUP FINELY CHOPPED SHALLOTS

¼ CUP FINELY CHOPPED SCALLIONS

¼ CUP COARSELY CHOPPED FRESH PARSLEY

½ CUP OLIVE OIL

2 CLOVES GARLIC, MINCED

½ TEASPOON SALT

½ TEASPOON COARSELY GROUND BLACK PEPPER

2 TABLESPOONS OLIVE OIL

½ CUP FINELY CHOPPED SHALLOTS

2 CUPS FRESH MUSHROOMS (LARGE ONES HALVED)

1 CUP HOMEMADE BEEF STOCK OR CANNED BROTH

½ TEASPOON FINELY CHOPPED FRESH SAGE LEAVES

½ TEASPOON SALT

½ TEASPOON GROUND BLACK PEPPER

FRESH WATERCRESS SPRIGS, FOR GARNISH

Combine the marinade ingredients in a small bowl and pour over the filets. Cover and refrigerate for at least 3 hours, turning once.

Remove the filets from the refrigerator and pat dry with paper towels. Heat 1 tablespoon of the oil in a large skillet, and sauté the shallots over medium heat until they have softened and are turning golden brown. Add the mushrooms and cook for 5 minutes, until they are tender. Stir in the stock, sage, salt, and pepper. Bring to a boil and reduce by about ¼ cup. Transfer the sauce to a heatproof bowl and keep warm.

In the same skillet heat the remaining tablespoon of oil over high heat, and cook the filets mignons according to taste. Transfer them to a serving platter, and pour the sauce over them or serve it separately. Garnish with watercress.

Serves 4

side dishes

PIGEON PEAS AND RICE

I was introduced to this dish, which is tremendously popular with my Jamaican friends, while traveling through the Caribbean. I adopted it as my own, and now it shows up on my table quite often.

2	TABLESPOONS OLIVE OIL
1	CUP CHOPPED ONIONS
4	CUPS HOMEMADE CHICKEN STOCK OR CANNED BROTH
2	BAY LEAVES
1	CUP PIGEON PEAS, SOAKED ACCORDING TO PACKAGE DIRECTIONS, RINSED, AND DRAINED
2	CUPS LONG-GRAIN RICE
2	TABLESPOONS JERK SEASONING (SEE PAGE 92)
1½	TEASPOONS SALT

Heat the oil in a large saucepan, and sauté the onions over medium heat until softened. Stir in the chicken stock, bay leaves, and pigeon peas, and bring to a boil. Reduce the heat, cover the pan, and cook for 45 minutes or until the pigeon peas are almost tender.

Add the rice, jerk seasoning, and salt. Cover and cook for another 15 to 20 minutes or until the rice is tender, adding more water to the pan if necessary. Remove bay leaves and serve immediately.

Makes about 7 cups (Serves 8 to 10)

BOURBON CORN PUDDING

Corn pudding turned up at most of our family holiday meals. My mother used a combination of canned whole-kernel corn and cream-style corn. I like to use corn right off the cob if it's in season. And you can add a spike of bourbon to taste.

2	LARGE EGGS
¾	CUP EVAPORATED MILK
2	CUPS CANNED CREAM-STYLE CORN
2	CUPS CORN KERNELS, CANNED (DRAINED), FROZEN (THAWED), OR FRESH
2	TABLESPOONS UNSALTED BUTTER, MELTED
2	TABLESPOONS DARK BROWN SUGAR
2	TABLESPOONS CORNSTARCH MIXED WITH 2 TABLESPOONS WATER
½	TEASPOON GROUND NUTMEG
3	TABLESPOONS BOURBON (OPTIONAL)
¼	TEASPOON SALT
¼	TEASPOON GROUND WHITE PEPPER

Preheat the oven to 350° F. Butter a 1-quart baking dish.

Beat the eggs and cream together in a large bowl. Stir in all the remaining ingredients, and pour the mixture into the baking dish. Bake for 45 minutes or until slightly browned and a fork inserted in the center comes out clean. Serve immediately.

Serves 6

Page 153: *Mango Chutney*

SAUTÉED GREEN PEPPERS AND TOMATOES

My mother made this dish with peppers and tomatoes that came from our garden. I've eliminated the sugar she used to put in her version, and I substitute sun-dried tomatoes for a touch of sweetness.

 3 TABLESPOONS SESAME OIL, OLIVE OIL, OR BACON DRIPPINGS
 4 LARGE GREEN BELL PEPPERS, SEEDED AND CUT INTO ½-INCH-WIDE SLICES (ABOUT 4 CUPS)
 4 LARGE TOMATOES, SEEDED AND CUT INTO ½-INCH-THICK SLICES (ABOUT 3 CUPS)
 ¼ CUP DRAINED AND FINELY SLICED SUN-DRIED TOMATOES IN OLIVE OIL
 ½ TEASPOON SALT
 ¼ TEASPOON GROUND BLACK PEPPER

Heat the oil in a large skillet and sauté the peppers over medium heat until softened. Add the fresh and sun-dried tomatoes, and cook for 2 to 3 minutes. Stir in the salt and pepper, and serve immediately.

Makes about 6 cups (Serves 5 to 6)

PAPRIKA ROASTED POTATOES

These unpeeled Red Bliss potatoes take on even more color with the addition of paprika. If you want a slightly incendiary effect, try using hot Hungarian paprika.

 4 CUPS RED BLISS POTATOES, UNPEELED, SCRUBBED, AND CUT INTO I-INCH CUBES
 ¼ CUP OLIVE OIL
 I TABLESPOON CHOPPED FRESH ROSEMARY, OR I ½ TEASPOONS CRUSHED DRIED
 I TEASPOON PAPRIKA
 ½ TEASPOON SALT
 ½ TEASPOON GROUND BLACK PEPPER

Combine all the ingredients in a large roasting pan and toss thoroughly to coat the potatoes with the seasonings. Cover with plastic wrap and let marinate for 30 minutes. Meanwhile, preheat the oven to 350° F.

Uncover the pan and roast the potatoes for 35 to 40 minutes, until they are golden and crisp. Serve immediately.

Makes 4 cups (Serves 4)

TOMATO SALSA

This diced vegetable mixture adds color to the plate and flavor to the food. It works as a side dish with meat and vegetables or—by adding some tomato sauce and extra jalapeño—as a Mexican dip to eat with chips.

1½	CUPS DICED SEEDED PLUM TOMATOES
½	CUP CHOPPED RED ONION
½	CUP FINELY CHOPPED CELERY
¼	CUP FINELY CHOPPED SCALLIONS
¼	CUP OLIVE OIL
2	TABLESPOONS BALSAMIC VINEGAR
1	TABLESPOON FRESH LEMON JUICE
1	TABLESPOON CHOPPED FRESH CILANTRO
½	TEASPOON SALT
¼	TEASPOON GROUND BLACK PEPPER
2	TABLESPOONS FINELY CHOPPED JALAPEÑO PEPPER (OPTIONAL)

Place all the ingredients in a large bowl and stir to thoroughly combine. Cover and chill until ready to serve.

Makes about 2½ cups

CINNAMON FRIED APPLES

There was an apple tree right outside our kitchen window. It was great for climbing and had excellent fruit. Mom made pies and canned apples, but it was her cinnamon fried apples we were all crazy about!

4	FIRM TART RED OR GREEN APPLES
2	TABLESPOONS UNSALTED BUTTER
½	CUP DARK BROWN SUGAR
⅛	TEASPOON GROUND CINNAMON

Rinse, core, and slice the apples. Heat the butter in a large skillet and add the apple slices. Cook for 3 to 4 minutes over medium heat, turning once. Stir in the brown sugar and cinnamon and cook for another 3 to 4 minutes, until the apples are golden and soft but not mushy.

Makes 2 cups (Serves 4)

MANGO OR PAPAYA CHUTNEY

Exotic foods are becoming so mainstream! Rooted in Caribbean culture, papayas and mangoes can be found in your neighborhood supermarket. I serve this chutney with poultry and seafood. It was on the menu, along with jerk duckling, at our wedding dinner. Make up a batch—it keeps well in the refrigerator and also makes a wonderful gift.

2	TABLESPOONS OLIVE OIL
½	CUP CHOPPED ONION
3	TABLESPOONS GRATED FRESH GINGER
2	CUPS CHOPPED FRESH MANGO OR PAPAYA (½-INCH CUBES)
1	CUP DARK BROWN SUGAR
½	TEASPOON DRIED RED PEPPER FLAKES
½	TEASPOON SALT
¾	CUP WATER
¼	CUP FINELY CHOPPED SCALLIONS

Heat the oil in a large skillet and sauté the onion over medium heat until softened. Stir in the ginger, mango or papaya, brown sugar, red pepper flakes, salt, and water. Bring to a boil, reduce the heat, and simmer for 35 to 40 minutes or until the fruit is very soft. Stir in the scallions and cook for another 5 minutes. Remove from the heat and let cool. Chill until ready to serve.

Makes 2¾ cups

desserts and breads

PINEAPPLE UPSIDE-DOWN CAKE

When I was little I loved to help my mom make this dessert. I especially liked the part when the cake came out of the oven and was expertly flipped over to reveal the rings of pineapple—intact and cherry-centered. It looked like a work of art. It still does!

TOPPING

¼ CUP UNSALTED BUTTER, MELTED

½ CUP FIRMLY PACKED LIGHT BROWN SUGAR

7 SLICES CANNED PINEAPPLE (RESERVE ½ CUP JUICE FOR THE CAKE)

13 CANDIED CHERRIES

CAKE

2 CUPS ALL-PURPOSE FLOUR

2 TEASPOONS BAKING POWDER

½ TEASPOON BAKING SODA

½ TEASPOON SALT

1 TEASPOON GROUND GINGER

¼ TEASPOON GROUND CLOVES

½ CUP UNSALTED BUTTER, SOFTENED

1 CUP SUGAR

2 LARGE EGGS

½ CUP HEAVY CREAM

½ CUP RESERVED PINEAPPLE JUICE

WHIPPED CREAM, FOR GARNISH

Preheat the oven to 350° F. Grease the sides of a 9 x 3-inch round baking pan with nonstick cooking spray or melted butter.

For the topping: Beat the melted butter and the brown sugar together in a small bowl. Spread this over the bottom of the prepared baking pan. Arrange 6 pineapple slices around the edge of the pan and one slice in the middle. Place a cherry in the center of each pineapple slice, and the rest between the slices around the edge.

To make the cake: Stir together the flour, baking powder, baking soda, salt, ginger, and cloves in a large bowl. In another large bowl, beat together the butter and sugar until light and fluffy. Beat in the eggs, one at a time. Using a spatula, alternately fold in the flour mixture and the heavy cream and pineapple juice until blended. Spread the batter over the pineapple slices, and bake for 1 hour or until a toothpick inserted in the center comes out clean.

Let the cake cool in the pan for 5 minutes. Then run a metal spatula around the edge to loosen the cake, invert a serving plate over the cake pan, and turn the cake and plate over together. Remove the cake pan. Serve warm, with whipped cream.

Makes one 9-inch cake (Serves 8 to 10)

PEACH COBBLER

Putting together a cobbler is a fun and easy alternative to the scary perfectionism of pie making. The peach filling can be prepared a day in advance, and if fresh or preserved peaches aren't available, the frozen variety will work just fine.

FILLING

6	LARGE RIPE PEACHES, PEELED AND PITTED, THICKLY SLICED (ABOUT 6 CUPS)
⅔	CUP FIRMLY PACKED DARK BROWN SUGAR
1	TABLESPOON CORNSTARCH
1	TEASPOON FRESH LEMON JUICE
½	TEASPOON GROUND CINNAMON
½	TEASPOON GROUND NUTMEG

BISCUIT TOPPING

1½	CUPS ALL-PURPOSE FLOUR
¼	CUP PLUS 1 TABLESPOON SUGAR
1½	TEASPOONS BAKING POWDER
½	TEASPOON SALT
¼	CUP UNSALTED BUTTER, CHILLED
⅔	CUP MILK
½	TEASPOON VANILLA EXTRACT

Preheat the oven to 375° F. Grease a 2-quart baking dish.

Combine the peaches, brown sugar, cornstarch, lemon juice, cinnamon, and nutmeg in a large saucepan. Mix gently, and cook over low heat until the peaches are just tender and the syrup has thickened, about 10 minutes. Pour the filling into the prepared baking dish.

Stir together the flour, ¼ cup sugar, baking powder, and salt in a large bowl. Using two knives or a pastry blender, cut in the butter until the mixture resembles coarse crumbs. Add the milk and vanilla, and quickly blend together with a spatula. Drop heaping tablespoons of the biscuit mixture on top of the peaches, covering them completely. Sprinkle with the remaining tablespoon sugar.

Bake for 25 to 30 minutes, until the top is golden and the biscuits are cooked through. Let the cobbler stand for 5 minutes before serving.

Serves 6

CRANBERRY BREAD PUDDING WITH BOURBON CUSTARD AND CRANBERRY SAUCE

You can of course make this dessert anytime, but I particularly love it in the fall and winter months because the bread and bourbon combination makes for a warm and hearty treat. Served plain and toasted, this also makes a wonderful breakfast bread.

¾	CUP HALF-AND-HALF
¾	CUP MILK
3	TABLESPOONS UNSALTED BUTTER
1	TEASPOON VANILLA EXTRACT
2	TEASPOONS GROUND CINNAMON
½	TEASPOON GROUND NUTMEG
2	LARGE EGGS
½	CUP SUGAR
12-14	LARGE SLICES WHITE BREAD, CRUSTS REMOVED, CUT INTO 1-INCH CUBES (6 CUPS)
¾	CUP FRESH OR FROZEN (THAWED) CRANBERRIES
¼	CUP CHOPPED PECANS, TOASTED
1	TABLESPOON UNSALTED BUTTER

2   LARGE EGG WHITES, LIGHTLY BEATEN
    BOURBON CUSTARD (RECIPE FOLLOWS)
    CRANBERRY SAUCE (RECIPE FOLLOWS)

Preheat the oven to 350° F. Grease a 9 x 5-inch loaf pan with nonstick cooking spray or melted butter.

Heat the half-and-half, milk, the 3 tablespoons of butter, vanilla, cinnamon, and nutmeg together in a large saucepan just until bubbles form around the edge of the pan. Remove from the heat.

Beat the eggs in a medium-size bowl. Beat in the sugar. Slowly pour about 1 cup of the scalded milk mixture into the eggs, whisking as you pour to prevent the eggs from cooking. Pour the egg mixture back into the saucepan. Add the bread cubes, cranberries, and pecans. Stir until thoroughly mixed. Pour the mixture into the prepared loaf pan and bake for 30 to 35 minutes, or until a toothpick inserted in the center comes out clean.

Cool the bread pudding in the pan. Then cover it with foil and refrigerate until ready to serve.

To serve: Remove the bread from the pan and cut the chilled loaf into 12 slices (about 3/4-inch-thick). Melt the 1 tablespoon butter in a large skillet over medium-high heat. Dip each side of several pudding slices in beaten egg white, and cook for 2 to 3 minutes per side, until golden and crispy. Keep them warm while you cook the remaining slices. Spoon some Bourbon Custard onto each dessert plate, arrange 2 slices of bread pudding in the center, and top with Cranberry Sauce. Serve immediately.

Serves 6

BOURBON CUSTARD

4   LARGE EGG YOLKS
½   CUP MAPLE SYRUP
1   TEASPOON VANILLA EXTRACT
1¼ CUPS HALF-AND-HALF
1   TABLESPOON UNSALTED BUTTER
2   TABLESPOONS BOURBON (OPTIONAL)

Whisk together the egg yolks, maple syrup, and vanilla in a small bowl. Heat the half-and-half in a medium-size heavy saucepan until bubbles form around the edge of the pan. Whisk a little of the cream into the egg yolk mixture; then pour this back into the pan. Cook over low heat, whisking occasionally, until the mixture thickens (10 to 15 minutes). Do not allow the mixture to boil or it will curdle. Stir in the butter and bourbon, and let it cool slightly. Refrigerate until ready to serve.

Makes 1²/3 cups

CRANBERRY SAUCE

2   CUPS FRESH OR FROZEN (THAWED)
    CRANBERRIES
¾   CUP SUGAR
¼   CUP WATER

Combine the cranberries, sugar, and water in a medium-size saucepan, and cook over low heat, stirring occasionally, until the sugar has dissolved. Increase the heat to medium and bring to a boil. Simmer for 10 minutes, until most of the berries have "popped." Remove from the heat and allow to cool. Refrigerate until ready to serve.

Makes 1 cup

Coconut Tuiles with Raspberry Coulis

Tuiles are thin delicate cookies that are shaped into cups after baking. People often end up playing with this dessert as their fingers invariably begin to snap off bits of the crispy tuiles. There is something very gratifying about being able to eat the container your food comes in! I often fill these with vanilla ice cream, but the options are unlimited.

½	CUP SUGAR
2	LARGE EGGS
¼	CUP ALL-PURPOSE FLOUR
¾	CUP UNSWEETENED SHREDDED COCONUT
	RASPBERRY COULIS (RECIPE FOLLOWS)
4	CUPS ICE CREAM OR MOUSSE
	TOASTED SHREDDED COCONUT, FOR GARNISH

Preheat the oven to 350° F. Brush a large baking sheet generously with melted butter.

Stir the sugar, eggs, flour, and coconut together in a medium-size bowl until well blended. Chill for 10 minutes.

Drop 2 large spoonfuls (2 heaping tablespoons each) of the chilled batter onto the prepared baking sheet. Spread each spoonful out to form a disc about 5 inches in diameter. Bake for 8 to 10 minutes, until the edges are golden brown.

Using a spatula, quickly ease each tuile off the baking sheet and place the top of the cookie over an upside-down custard cup. Repeat with the remaining batter, brushing the sheet with melted butter each time. Leave the tuiles over the cup until they are completely cooled and firm.

Store the tuiles in a single layer in an airtight container in a cool place to prevent them from softening (they are very sensitive to humid conditions). They may also be frozen for up to 1 month.

To serve: Spoon a little Raspberry Coulis on each dessert plate, place a tuile in the center, and carefully fill the tuile with about $1/2$ cup ice cream or mousse. Drizzle a teaspoon of the coulis over the ice cream, and sprinkle with a little toasted shredded coconut, if desired. Serve immediately.

Makes 8 tuiles

RASPBERRY COULIS

3	CUPS FRESH OR FROZEN (THAWED) RASPBERRIES
½	CUP WATER
⅓	CUP CONFECTIONERS' SUGAR, SIFTED

Combine the raspberries and the water in a blender or food processor, and purée until smooth. Strain through a sieve to remove the seeds. Stir in the confectioners' sugar until blended. Refrigerate until ready to serve.

Makes $1\,3/4$ cups

Flourless Chocolate Nut Torte

I was first introduced to this melt-in-your-mouth torte while living in Austria and marveled at the fact that it does not contain flour. Frau Jecel, my friend's mother, would make it for late-afternoon tea and coffee and serve it *mit Schlag*—with fresh whipped cream.

TORTE

5	LARGE EGGS, SEPARATED
¾	CUP SUGAR

¼ CUP UNSWEETENED COCOA POWDER

PINCH OF BAKING SODA

2 CUPS FINELY GROUND TOASTED HAZELNUTS

OR ALMONDS (ABOUT 8 OUNCES)

¼ CUP FINE UNSEASONED DRIED BREAD CRUMBS

1 TABLESPOON CRÈME DE CACAO

GLAZE

4 OUNCES (4 SQUARES) SEMISWEET BAKING

CHOCOLATE, CHOPPED

3 TABLESPOONS UNSALTED BUTTER

1 TABLESPOON LIGHT CORN SYRUP

Preheat the oven to 350° F. Grease the bottom and sides of a 9-inch round springform cake pan. Cut a disc of parchment paper to fit the bottom, and grease that as well.

Using an electric beater on medium-high speed, whip the egg yolks with the sugar until the mixture is very thick, pale, and creamy (this takes about 5 minutes). Stir the cocoa powder and baking soda together, and sift this over the egg yolk mixture. Using a spatula, fold the ground nuts, bread crumbs, crème de cacao, and cocoa powder into the egg yolks.

Using clean beaters, beat the egg whites with the electric mixer until they are stiff. Fold one third of the egg whites into the yolk mixture until well blended. Gently fold the yolk mixture into the whites.

Pour the mixture into the prepared pan and bake for 30 to 35 minutes, until the cake is well risen and a toothpick inserted in the center comes out clean. Remove the cake from the oven and run a spatula around the edge to loosen it; let it cool in the pan for 15 minutes. Then remove the cake from the pan and allow it to cool completely on a rack.

To make the glaze: Melt the chocolate with the butter in a small saucepan over very low heat. Remove the pan from the heat and stir in the corn syrup. Pour the glaze over the cooled cake and let it set before serving, about 30 minutes.

Makes one 9-inch cake (Serves 6 to 8)

MINCEMEAT MUFFINS

When I was in junior high school, it was my job to get up early and prepare muffins for breakfast. I still like to start my day with fresh muffins. I usually have a jar of mincemeat on hand, and it makes a great sweet addition to the muffins.

1¾ CUPS ALL-PURPOSE FLOUR

¼ CUP FIRMLY PACKED DARK BROWN SUGAR

2 TEASPOONS BAKING POWDER

¼ TEASPOON BAKING SODA

¼ TEASPOON SALT

¾ CUP MILK

¼ CUP UNSALTED BUTTER, MELTED

1 LARGE EGG

1 CUP MINCEMEAT

Preheat the oven to 375° F. Grease 12 muffin cups or line them with paper muffin cups.

In a large bowl, stir together the flour, brown sugar, baking powder, baking soda, and salt. In another bowl, whisk together the milk, melted butter, and egg. Stir the milk mixture into the dry ingredients, and then gently fold in the mincemeat. Divide the batter among the muffin cups. Bake for 15 to 20 minutes, or until the muffins are well risen and a toothpick comes out clean when inserted in the center.

Makes 12 muffins

VOLCANIC SCONES

Dan came up with the name for these wake-up-your-mouth scones that are great to eat any time. It's the cayenne pepper and the chili powder that make these so wonderfully incendiary.

2	CUPS ALL-PURPOSE FLOUR
1	TABLESPOON BAKING POWDER
1	TEASPOON SUGAR
1	TEASPOON SALT
½	TEASPOON CHILI POWDER
½	TEASPOON GARLIC POWDER
½	TEASPOON ONION POWDER
½	TEASPOON DRIED THYME
½	TEASPOON CARAWAY SEED
¼	TEASPOON POWDERED DRIED SAGE
¼	TEASPOON CAYENNE PEPPER
½	CUP UNSALTED BUTTER, CHILLED
½	CUP MILK
1	LARGE EGG

Preheat the oven to 400° F. Grease and flour a large baking sheet.

In a large bowl, stir together the flour, baking powder, sugar, salt, and all the herbs and spices. Using two knives or a pastry blender, cut in the butter until the mixture resembles coarse crumbs. Whisk the milk and egg together in a small bowl, and stir this into the flour mixture to form a soft dough. Turn the dough out onto a floured surface and lightly knead it just until smooth.

Pat the dough out to form a 12-inch square, and cut it into 12 squares. Place them on the baking sheet, and bake for 10 to 12 minutes or until golden. Transfer to a wire rack to cool.

Variation: Before baking, brush the scones with beaten egg and sprinkle them with salt.

Makes 12 scones

ST. LUCIA BANANA BREAD

The island of St. Lucia, where Dan and I attended the St. Lucia Jazz Festival, grows the best-tasting bananas I've ever eaten. I won't advise you to smuggle this fruit in, but do use the softest, ripest bananas you can find when you make this bread.

1 ½	CUPS ALL-PURPOSE FLOUR
1	TEASPOON BAKING SODA
1	TEASPOON SALT
½	TEASPOON GROUND NUTMEG
½	TEASPOON GROUND CINNAMON
¼	TEASPOON GROUND ALLSPICE
½	CUP UNSALTED BUTTER, SOFTENED
½	CUP SUGAR
½	CUP FIRMLY PACKED LIGHT BROWN SUGAR
2	LARGE EGGS
1 ¼	CUPS MASHED RIPE BANANA
½	CUP "LIGHT" SOUR CREAM
1	TEASPOON VANILLA EXTRACT
½	CUP CHOPPED WALNUTS OR PECANS
¼	CUP CHOPPED DATES OR DRIED APRICOTS (OPTIONAL)

Preheat the oven to 350° F. Grease a 9 x 5-inch loaf pan.

In a large bowl, stir together the flour, baking soda, salt, nutmeg, cinnamon, and allspice. In another large bowl, beat the butter and sugars until light. Beat in the eggs, one at a time. Then fold in the flour mixture, alternating with the mashed banana, sour cream, and vanilla. Stir in the nuts, and the dates or apricots if you are using them. Pour the batter into the loaf pan and bake for 1 hour, or until a toothpick inserted in the center comes out clean. Transfer the bread to a wire rack to cool.

Makes 1 loaf

B. SMITH'S YEAST ROLLS

My Grandmother Hart made these rolls all the time. She would knead a big batch of dough, then put it on the heating grate and cover it with a towel. I'd watch the dough rise and see her punch it down over and over—a process that resulted in these tasty, fragrant rolls.

2	PACKAGES ACTIVE DRY YEAST
3	CUPS WATER WARMED (105 TO 115 F)
1	TABLESPOON SALT
7½-8½	CUPS BREAD FLOUR
	CORNMEAL
1	LARGE EGG, BEATEN WITH 1 TABLESPOON WATER

Stir the yeast into the warm water in a large mixing bowl until dissolved. Stir in salt. Add 7½ cups of the flour and stir until a dough is formed. Turn the dough out onto a floured surface and knead until it is smooth, adding a tablespoon of flour at a time if necessary to make a soft but not sticky dough.

Place the dough in a greased bowl, turning it once to coat the top with grease. Cover the bowl loosely with plastic wrap. Turn oven on lowest setting for 1 minute. Turn off. Place the bowl in the oven and let the dough rise about 1½ hours or until doubled in size. Meanwhile, grease two baking sheets and sprinkle cornmeal over them.

Gently punch down the dough. Cut it into 32 pieces, shape them into rolls, and arrange them on the baking sheets. Cover as above and let rise in oven or warm place for 30 minutes, until doubled in size again. Remove rolls from the oven.

Preheat the oven to 375° F.

Brush the tops of the rolls with the beaten egg and bake for 30 minutes, until they are crusty and the bottoms sound hollow when tapped. Transfer the rolls to wire racks to cool completely.

Makes 32 rolls

Variation: This is the dough I use for my Disappearing Cinnamon Rolls (recipe follows). If you like, divide the dough in half and make 16 yeast rolls and 12 cinnamon rolls.

DISAPPEARING CINNAMON ROLLS

Whenever I bake these, Dan and Dana go into a frenzy because the whole house is filled with the smell of baking bread combined with the irresistible aroma of cinnamon. Once out of the oven, the rolls are never around for very long.

1	CUP FIRMLY PACKED DARK BROWN SUGAR
½	CUP RAISINS
½	CUP CHOPPED WALNUTS
¼	CUP UNSALTED BUTTER, MELTED
1	TEASPOON GROUND CINNAMON
½	BATCH DOUGH FOR B. SMITH'S YEAST ROLLS (LEFT)

Mix the brown sugar, raisins, walnuts, melted butter, and cinnamon together in a small bowl. Butter a 9-inch round cake pan.

Prepare the Yeast Roll dough and let it go through the first rising (about 1¹/₂ hours). Punch down the dough, and roll it out on a floured surface to form a 12 x 9-inch rectangle. Spread the filling over the dough, leaving a ¹/₄-inch border all the way around. Working from the long side, roll the dough up to form a 12-inch-long roll. Cut it into 12 slices, and place them together tightly in the cake pan. Cover loosely with plastic wrap and let rise in a warm place for 30 minutes or until doubled in size.

Preheat the oven to 400° F.

Bake the rolls for 25 minutes, or until well risen and golden brown. Let them cool in the pan for 10 minutes before turning them out onto a wire rack to cool completely.

Makes 12 rolls

WHOLE WHEAT POTATO ROLLS

I don't remember whole wheat flour from my childhood, but I do recall my father preaching about the importance of vitamins and eating right. These rolls, which also contain mashed potatoes, come from an old recipe that stands the test of our health-conscious times.

1	LARGE POTATO (12 OUNCES), PEELED AND CUBED
4	TEASPOONS ACTIVE DRY YEAST
1	TABLESPOON SUGAR
2¾	CUPS ALL-PURPOSE FLOUR
2¼	CUPS WHOLE WHEAT FLOUR
1½	TEASPOONS SALT
⅔	CUP MILK, WARMED (105 TO 115 F)
2	LARGE EGGS, LIGHTLY BEATEN
2	TABLESPOONS UNSALTED BUTTER, MELTED

Cook the potato in boiling salted water until tender. Drain, reserving ¹/₄ cup of the cooking liquid, and mash the potato well. Set it aside.

Cool the reserved potato cooking liquid to between 105° and 115° F. Then stir the yeast and the sugar into the liquid and let the mixture stand until it is frothy (about 10 minutes). Meanwhile, stir the flours and salt together in a large bowl.

In a large mixing bowl, stir together the yeast mixture, warm milk, eggs, melted butter, and mashed potato. Add 3 cups of the flour mixture and beat for 5 minutes, until very smooth. Gradually add more of the flour mixture to form a dough. Turn the dough out onto a floured surface, and gradually knead in the remaining flour. Continue to knead the dough until it is smooth. It should be soft but not sticky. If necessary add more flour, 1 tablespoon at a time.

Place the dough in a large greased bowl, and turn it over once to coat the top with grease. Cover the bowl loosely with greased plastic wrap, and let the dough rise in a warm place for 1 hour or until it has doubled in size.

Grease 12 large muffin cups. Punch the dough down and divide it into 12 pieces. Shape them into smooth rounds and place them in the muffin cups (or if you like, divide each round into 3 small balls and place them in each muffin cup to form clover-shaped rolls). Cover as before, and let rise in a warm place for 30 minutes or until doubled in size. Meanwhile, preheat the oven to 400° F.

Bake the rolls for 15 to 20 minutes, until they are golden on top and sound hollow when tapped on the bottom. Transfer them to a wire rack to cool completely.

Makes 12 rolls

ACKNOWLEDGMENTS

I'd like to express my sincere thanks and appreciation to the many wonderful people who have helped make this book possible: my literary agent, Marie Dutton Brown, for her foresight, vision, and patience; Leslie Stoker, my editor at Artisan, who believed in me wholeheartedly and guided me with her knowledge, dedication, and high standards; Bill Lalor, who helped me develop my early restaurant food ideas; Henry Chung, my chef at B. Smith's New York, for our years of sharing food experiences together; Kathleen Cromwell, my new friend and collaborator, for her talent, funky style, and love of life; Helene Silverman for her imaginative, appealing design; the photography team of Gentl & Hyers and their assistants for the beauty of their photography; photographer Jennifer Levy and food stylist Joanne Rubin, and Fran Black for introducing them to me and for her undying support of this project; recipe tester Carol Harlem and culinary troubleshooter Rhonda Stieglitz; Kathie Ness for her expert copy editing; prop stylists and all-around talents, Edward Peterson and Kemper Hyers, whose creativity, enthusiasm, and ability to remain calm under pressure were a constant inspiration to me.

Thank you also to all my friends who took the time out from busy schedules to participate in the entertaining sections, including Joe and Eve Sanabria, Lorraine Foxworth, Jonathan Brown, Andrea Fischman Khalila, Rebecca and Henry Young, Larry Carr, Rachel and Terry Epstein, Valerie and Erica Beal, Clarice Taylor, and Kathy Sharpton; Jose and Ayishah Ferrer of The Kwanzaa Foundation, Stephanie Sills, Jasperdine Kobes, and Frank Wimberly; Eric Robertson and C. Julian Clark for their beautiful artwork; Barbara and Earl Graves for the use of their bay view; Sherry Bronfman, her family, and staff for opening up her beautiful home to us and lending her elegance to our photo shoot; Bill Karg, Reese Fayde, and children Banchamlak and Habtamu, for opening up their home/gallery for our cocktail party.

I am grateful to Nyieta Hedrington, Alex Morrison, Helen Claydon-Way, and the staff and management of B. Smith's restaurant; Robert Stein, Esq. and Ira Goldstein, Esq.

A special thanks to Leah Feldon and Nancy Doll, all my gal pals and sisters, my husband, my stepdaughter, my family.

To Workman Publishing, thanks.

CREDITS

Page 11: glasses courtesy of Möet et Chandon Champagne; Pages 12–18: glassware courtesy of Takashimaya (800/753-2038 or in New York City 212/350-0100) and Pottery Barn (800/922-5507); Page 21: plate courtesy of Pottery Barn, glass bowl courtesy of Bergdorf Goodman (800/967-3788 or in New York City 212/752-7300); Page 22: platter courtesy of ABC Carpet & Home (800/888-7847 or in New York City 212/473-3000); Page 25: napkin, cloth, and plates courtesy of ABC Carpet & Home; Page 27: plate courtesy of Wolfman Gold & Good Company (800/862-2288 or in New York City 212/431-1888); Pages 29–33: damask runner and silver heart bowl courtesy of Maison Moderne (212/691-1603); Page 36: napkin courtesy of ABC Carpet & Home; Page 41: Lalique decanter courtesy of Takashimaya, fork courtesy of Pottery Barn; Page 42: plate by Johnson Brothers (available at fine china boutiques); Pages 44–46: ribbed glass pitcher courtesy of Metropolitan Museum of Art Gift Shop (800/468-7386), wooden tray courtesy of Pottery Barn, small white ribbed bowl courtesy of Dean and Delucca (212/431-1691), iron thongs courtesy of Pottery Barn; Pages 63–71: plates courtesy of Taitu "Noel" (P.O. Box 58090, Dallas TX 75258 for information), glassware, mats, and napkins courtesy of Macintosh Tabletop at Henri Bendel (212/247-1100); Page 77: Plate courtesy of Takashimaya; Page 80: candle holder courtesy of Kwanzaa Foundation, mud cloth wall hanging courtesy of Eric Robertson Gallery of African Art (212/675-4045), bowls, trays, and baskets courtesy of Bamboula Associates (212/675-2714); Pages 82–84: mats, wooden tray, napkins, and napkin rings courtesy of Bamboula Associates, plates courtesy of Pottery Barn, glassware courtesy of Williams–Sonoma (800/541-2233); page 87: large spoon courtesy of Takashimaya, bowl courtesy of Wolfman Gold & Good Company; Page 88: basket courtesy of Pottery Barn; Page 90: linens courtesy of ABC Carpet & Home; Page 94: large plate courtesy of Wolfman Gold & Good Company, cloth courtesy of Bamboula; Page 99: linen cloth courtesy of ABC Carpet & Home; Page 103: platter courtesy of Wolfman Gold & Good Company; Page 108: table courtesy of ABC Carpet & Home, linen courtesy of Broadway Panhandler (212/966-3434); Page 112: linen cloth courtesy of Takashimaya; Page 117: mat courtesy of Pottery Barn, plate courtesy of Bergdorf Goodman, glass courtesy of Willams–Sonoma; Page 122–124: apron courtesy of Broadway Panhandler; Page 127: bowl courtesy of ABC Carpet & Home, linen courtesy of Broadway Panhandler; Page 135: plate courtesy of ABC Carpet & Home; Page 147: linen courtesy of Broadway Panhandler; Page 149: table courtesy of ABC Carpet & Home, mallet courtesy of Broadway Panhandler; Page 151: plate, fork, and glass courtesy of Takashimaya, linen courtesy of ABC Carpet & Home; Page 154: spoon courtesy of Takashimaya; Page 167: glass courtesy of Takashimaya, napkin courtesy of ABC Carpet & Home.

CONVERSION CHART

Volume Equivalents

These are not exact equivalents for the American cups and spoons, but have been rounded up or down slightly to make measuring easier.

American	Metric	Imperial
¼ t	1.25 ml	
½ t	2.5 ml	
1 t	5 ml	
½ T (1 ½ t)	7.5 ml	
1 T (3 t)	15 ml	
¼ cup (4 T)	60 ml	2 fl oz
⅓ cup (5 T)	75 ml	2 ½ fl oz
½ cup (8 T)	125 ml	4 fl oz
⅔ cup (10 T)	150 ml	5 fl oz (¼ pint)
¾ cup (12 T)	175 ml	6 fl oz
1 cup (16 T)	250 ml	8 fl oz
1 ¼ cups	300 ml	10 fl oz (½ pint)
1 ½ cups	350 ml	12 fl oz
1 pint (2 cups)	500 ml	16 fl oz
1 quart (4 cups)	1 litre	1 ¾ pints

Weight Equivalents

The metric weights given in this chart are not exact equivalents, but have been rounded up or down slightly to make measuring easier.

Avoirdupois	Metric
¼ oz	7 g
½ oz	15 g
1 oz	30 g
2 oz	60 g
3 oz	90 g
4 oz	115 g
5 oz	150 g
6 oz	175 g
7 oz	200 g
8 oz (½ lb)	225 g
9 oz	250 g
10 oz	300 g
11 oz	325 g
12 oz	350 g
13 oz	375 g
14 oz	400 g
15 oz	425 g
16 oz (1 lb)	450 g
1 lb 2 oz	500 g
1½ lb	750 g
2 lb	900 g
2 ¼ lb	1 kg
3 lb	1.4 kg
4 lb	1.8 kg
4 ½ lb	2 kg

Oven Temperature Equivalents

In the recipes in this book, only Fahrenheit temperatures have been given. Consult this chart for the Centigrade and gas mark equivalents.

Oven	° F.	° C.	Gas Mark
very cool	250–275	130–140	½–1
cool	300	150	2
warm	325	170	3
moderate	350	180	4
moderately hot	375	190	5
	400	200	6
hot	425	220	7
very hot	450	230	8
	475	250	9

INDEX

(Page numbers in italic
refer to illustrations.)

APPETIZERS, hors
    d'oeuvres, and first
    courses:
Cajun catfish fingers, 101
chitterlings in puff
    pastry, 101
curried vegetables in
    puff pastry, 70, 71
fresh pasta dough,
    122-23, 123
gingery chicken kabobs
    with honey mustard
    sauce, 22, 22
herbed onion tart, 100
marinated party lamb
    chops with mint dip, 26, 27
pan-fried crab cakes with
    chili mayonnaise, 23, 23
potato leek pancakes, 24, 24
salmon tartare, 99, 100
shrimp and plantains on
    skewers with mango
    mayonnaise, 21, 21
Vineyard lobster dip, 25, 25
see also Salads, first-course
    or side-dish
Apples, cinnamon fried, 157

BANANA:
    bread, St. Lucia, 166, 167
    hash, 93, 93
Bar, stocking of, 18, 19
Basil vinaigrette, 115
Beef, marinated filet
    mignon of, with
    mushrooms, 150, 151
Berry berry soup, 106
Beurre blanc, 134
Bitter greens with
    balsamic vinaigrette, 74
Black bean soup with
    andouille sausage and
    sour cream, 107
Black-eyed pea soup with
    smoked turkey, 86, 87
Bourbon:

corn pudding, 155
custard, 163
Bow-tie pasta with smoked
    salmon and dill, 128
Bread(s):
    banana, St. Lucia, 166, 167
    cornbread, 145
    jalapeño cornbread, 88, 89
    mincemeat muffins, 165
    pudding, cranberry,
        with bourbon custard
        and cranberry sauce,
        162-63
    volcanic scones, 166
    see also Rolls
Buffet arrangements,
    81-83, 84

CABBAGE, in spicy
    coleslaw, 114
Cajun catfish fingers, 101
Cakes (savory), pan-fried
    crab, with chili
    mayonnaise, 23, 23
Cakes (sweet):
    lemon pound, 60, 61
    pineapple upside-down,
        160, 161
    see also Tortes
Caribbean:
    grilled shrimp with
        mango glacé and
        plantains, 132, 133
    jerk duckling, 92
    seared tuna with coconut
        curry sauce, 134-35, 135
Catfish fingers, Cajun, 101
Champagne:
    fountain, 11, 11
    saffron cream, 140
Cheese:
    chèvre croutons, 36, 37
    macaroni and, old-
        fashioned baked, 126
Chèvre croutons, 36, 37
Chicken:
    cornbread pot pie,
        144, 145
    fried, Mom's, 146

kabobs, gingery, with
    honey mustard sauce,
    22, 22
soup, Henry's, 105
spinach fettuccine
    with, in spicy tomato
    sauce, 128
Chili(es):
    jalapeño corn bread, 88, 89
    mayonnaise, 23
Chitterlings, 146
    in puff pastry, 101
Chocolate:
    flourless nut torte,
        164-65
    glaze, 165
    mocha torte with crème
        anglaise and raspberry
        coulis, 42, 43
    sauce, 75
    strawberries dipped in, 33
Chowder, sweet corn and
    crab, 108, 109
Christmas celebration.
    see Kwanzaa/Christmas
    buffet
Chutney, mango or papaya,
    153, 157
Cinnamon:
    fried apples, 157
    rolls, disappearing,
        168-69
Citrus vinaigrette, 137
Clam sauce, spaghetti
    with, 129
Cobbler, peach, 162
Cocktail, Tribeca, 18
Cocktail party for
    business and
    pleasure, 12-27
    decorations for, 17
    invitations to, 15, 17
    length of, 14-15
    location for, 15-16
    menu for, 17, 18, 20
    quantity of food for, 17-18
    recipes for, 21-27
    serving of food at, 17
    social interaction at, 16

starting time of, 13-14
stocking bar for, 18, 19
Cocktails, before formal
    dinner, 68
Coconut:
    curry sauce, 134-35
    tuiles with raspberry
        coulis, 164
Coffee, 66
Coleslaw, spicy, 114
Corn:
    bourbon pudding, 155
    sweet, and crab
        chowder, 108, 109
Cornbread, 145
    chicken pot pie, 144, 145
    jalapeño, 88, 89
Cornish hens, rosemary
    roast, 72, 73
Cornmeal pan-fried
    whiting, 90, 90
Crab(s):
    cakes, pan-fried, with
        chili mayonnaise, 23, 23
    soft-shell, with lemon
        caper sauce, 141
    and sweet corn chowder,
        108, 109
Cranberry bread pudding
    with bourbon custard
    and cranberry sauce,
    162-63
Crème anglaise, 76
Croutons, chèvre, 36, 37
Curry(ied):
    coconut sauce, 134-35
    vegetables in puff
        pastry, 70, 71
Custard:
    bourbon, 163
    crème anglaise, 76

DECORATIONS, 17, 32, 53,
    83-84
Desserts, 66
    coconut tuiles with
        raspberry coulis, 164
    cranberry bread pudding
        with bourbon custard

and cranberry sauce,
162-63
flourless chocolate nut
torte, 164-65
lemon pound cake, 60, *61*
mocha torte with crème
anglaise and raspberry
coulis, *42, 43*
peach cobbler, 162
pineapple upside-down
cake, *160, 161*
profiteroles with
vanilla ice cream,
crème anglaise, and
chocolate sauce,
75-76, *76-77*
strawberries dipped in
chocolate, 33
sweet potato pie with
praline pecan sauce,
94, 95
Dijon dressing, 116
Dips:
mint, 26
spicy Cajun, 101
tomato salsa, 156-57
Vineyard lobster, *25, 25*
Dress, suggestions for,
15, 46-47
Dressings:
Dijon, 116
for fruit, 114
spicy sesame peanut, 115
see also Vinaigrettes
Duck(ling):
jerk, 92
sausage, *147, 147*

ENDIVE, tomato, and
watercress salad, 39
Exotic fruit salad, 114

FETTUCCINE, spinach, with
chicken in spicy
tomato sauce, 128
Filet mignon, marinated,
with mushrooms, 150, *151*
First courses. *See*
Appetizers, hors
d'oeuvres, and first
courses
Fish. *See* Salmon; Seafood
Flourless chocolate nut
torte, 164-65

Formal dinner, 62-77
beginning of, 68
dressing table for, 67, 68
ending of, 66-68
invitations to, 63-64
menu for, 69
music for, 65
number of guests at, 64
pace of, 65, 68
place cards for, 64-65
recipes for, 70-77
seating arrangements
for, 64, 65
service help for, 68
table shape for, 65
Fried chicken, Mom's, 146
Fruit salad, exotic, 114

GARLIC mashed potatoes, 74
Gazpacho, tangy, 56
Ginger(y):
chicken kabobs with
honey mustard sauce,
22, 22
orange sauce, 139
Greens:
bitter, with balsamic
vinaigrette, 74
warm mixed, salad, 91
Grilled:
marinated swordfish
steaks, 56, *57*
salmon salad with wild
mushrooms and roasted
potatoes, 116, *117*
seafood brochettes, 138
seafood salad, 138
shrimp with mango glacé
and plantains, *132, 133*
vegetables, herb-marinated,
58, 59
Grilling, 48, 54
Grouper with Champagne
saffron cream, 140

HERB:
beurre blanc, 134
marinade, 59
Honey:
mustard sauce, 22
mustard vinaigrette,
119
Hors d'oeuvres. *See*
Appetizers, hors

d'oeuvres, and first
courses

INVITATIONS, 15, 17, 32,
63-64

JALAPEÑO cornbread, *88, 89*
Jerk duckling, 92

KIDS:
picnic at beach for, 49-51
Valentine's dinner for, 33
Kwanzaa, 79-80, 81
Kwanzaa/Christmas
buffet, 78-95
activities for, 81
dress and decor for, 83-84
invitations to, 83
menu for, 84, 85
recipes for, 86-95
serving and eating
arrangements for,
81-83, 84

LAMB chops:
baby, with Madeira sauce,
35, 35
marinated party, with
mint dip, 26, *27*
Leek potato pancakes, *24, 24*
Lemon pound cake, 60, *61*
Lime vinaigrette, 138
Linguine with roasted
plum tomato sauce, 40, *41*
Lobster:
dip, Vineyard, *25, 25*
ravioli with tomato
cream sauce, *124, 125*

MACARONI and cheese, old-
fashioned baked, 126
Main dishes:
baby lamb chops with
Madeira sauce, *35, 35*
bow-tie pasta with
smoked salmon and
dill, 128
cornbread chicken pot
pie, *144, 145*
cornmeal pan-fried
whiting, 90, *90*
fillets of sole with
herbal beurre blanc, 134
flash-roasted salmon

with Swiss chard and
citrus vinaigrette, *136, 137*
fresh pasta, *122-23, 123*
grilled seafood
brochettes, 138
grilled shrimp with
mango glacé and
plantains, *132, 133*
grouper with Champagne
saffron cream, 140
jerk duckling, 92
linguine with roasted
plum tomato sauce, 40, *41*
lobster ravioli with
tomato cream sauce,
124, 125
marinated filet mignon
with mushrooms, 150, *151*
marinated grilled
swordfish steaks, 56, *57*
Mom's fried chicken, 146
old-fashioned baked
macaroni and cheese, 126
pasta primavera, 126
rigatoni with ground
veal and sage, 129
rosemary roast Cornish
hens, *72, 73*
sea bass with orange-
ginger sauce, 139
seared tuna with
coconut curry sauce,
134-35, 135
smothered pork chops, 148
soft-shell crabs with
lemon caper sauce, 141
spaghetti with clam
sauce, 129
spinach fettuccine with
chicken in spicy
tomato sauce, 128
veal chops with sage,
148, *149*
see also Salads, main-dish
Mango:
chutney, *153, 157*
exotic fruit salad, 114
glacé, 133
mayonnaise, 21
Marinades:
herb, 59
for meat, 26, 150
for poultry, 22, 73
for seafood, 56, 133, 138

Mayonnaise:
  chili, 23
  mango, 21
Melon soup, chilled
  mixed, *104, 105*
Mincemeat muffins, 165
Mint dip, 26
Mocha torte with crème
  anglaise and
  raspberry coulis, *42, 43*
Muffins:
  jalapeño corn, *88, 89*
  mincemeat, 165
Music, 32, 65
Mustard:
  Dijon dressing, 116
  honey sauce, 22
  honey vinaigrette, 119

OLIVE tapenade, 119
Onion tart, herbed, 100
Orange-ginger sauce, 139

PANCAKES, potato leek,
  24, 24
Papaya:
  chutney, 157
  exotic fruit salad, 114
Paprika roasted potatoes,
  156
Pasta:
  bow-tie, with smoked
    salmon and dill, 128
  fresh, dough, *122-23, 123*
  linguine with roasted
    plum tomato sauce,
    40, 41
  lobster ravioli with
    tomato cream sauce,
    124, 125
  old-fashioned baked
    macaroni and cheese, 126
  primavera, 126
  rigatoni with ground
    veal and sage, 129
  spaghetti with clam
    sauce, 129
  spinach fettuccine with
    chicken in spicy
    tomato sauce, 128
  tricolor, salad, *127, 127*
Pastry. *See* Puff pastry
Pea(s):
  black-eyed, with smoked

turkey, 86, *87*
pigeon, and rice, *154, 155*
summer green, salad,
  112, 113
Peach cobbler, 162
Peanut sesame dressing,
  spicy, 115
Pecan praline sauce, 95
Peppers:
  green, sautéed tomatoes
    and, 156
  see also Chili(es)
Picnic at the beach, 44-61
  contingency plans for,
    52-54
  "dress code" for, 46-47
  food preparation for,
    47-49, 51, 54
  for kids, 49-51
  grilling at, 48, 54
  menu for, 47, 55
  preparing site for, 53
  recipes for, 56-61
  trek to beach in, 52
Pies:
  cornbread chicken pot,
    144, 145
  sweet potato, with
    praline pecan sauce, *94, 95*
Pigeon peas and rice,
  154, 155
Pineapple:
  exotic fruit salad, 114
  upside-down cake, *160, 161*
Place cards, 33, 64-65
Plantains:
  banana hash, *93, 93*
  grilled shrimp with
    mango glacé and, *132, 133*
  and shrimp on skewers
    with mango
    mayonnaise, *21, 21*
Pork:
  chitterlings, 146
  chitterlings in puff
    pastry, 101
  chops, smothered, 148
Potato(es):
  garlic mashed, 74
  au gratin, 38
  leek pancakes, *24, 24*
  paprika roasted, 156
  salad, blissful, 118
  whole wheat rolls, 169

Pot pie, cornbread
  chicken, *144, 145*
Pound cake, lemon, 60,
  60-61
Praline pecan sauce, 95
Profiteroles with vanilla
  ice cream, crème
  anglaise, and
  chocolate sauce,
  75-76, 76-77
Psychological
  preparation, 51-52
Puddings:
  bourbon corn, 155
  cranberry bread, with
    bourbon custard and
    cranberry sauce, 162-63
Puff pastry:
  chitterlings in, 101
  curried vegetables in,
    70, 71

RASPBERRY:
  coulis, 164
  vinaigrette, 39
Ravioli, lobster, with
  tomato cream sauce,
  124, 125
Rice, pigeon peas and,
  154, 155
Rigatoni with ground veal
  and sage, 129
Rolls:
  disappearing cinnamon,
    168-69
  whole wheat potato, 169
  yeast, B. Smith's, 168
Romaine salad with basil
  vinaigrette, 115
Rosemary roast Cornish
  hens, *72, 73*

SAFFRON Champagne
  cream, 140
St. Lucia banana bread,
  166, 167
Salads, first-course or
  side-dish:
  bitter greens with
    balsamic vinaigrette, 74
  blissful potato, 118
  exotic fruit, 114
  olive tapenade, 119
  romaine, with basil

vinaigrette, 115
  spicy coleslaw, 114
  summer green pea,
    112, 113
  tomato, watercress, and
    endive, 39
  tricolor pasta, *127, 127*
  warm mixed greens, 91
Salads, main-dish:
  grilled salmon, with
    wild mushrooms and
    roasted potatoes, *116, 117*
  grilled seafood, 138
  warm mixed greens, 91
Salmon:
  flash-roasted, with
    Swiss chard and
    citrus vinaigrette, *136, 137*
  grilled, salad with
    wild mushrooms and
    roasted potatoes, *116, 117*
  smoked, bow-tie pasta
    with dill and, 128
  tartare, *99*, 100
Salsa, tomato, 156-57
Sauces (savory):
  beurre blanc, 134
  Champagne saffron
    cream, 140
  chili mayonnaise, 23
  coconut curry, 134-35
  honey mustard, 22
  mango glacé, 133
  mango mayonnaise, 21
  mint dip, 26
  orange-ginger, 139
  roasted plum tomato, 40
  tartar, 90
Sauces (sweet):
  chocolate, 75
  cranberry, 163
  praline pecan, 95
  raspberry coulis, 164
Sausage, duck, *147, 147*
Scallops, in grilled
  seafood brochettes, 138
Scones, volcanic, 166
Sea bass with orange-
  ginger sauce, 139
Seafood:
  Cajun catfish fingers, 101
  cornmeal pan-fried
    whiting, *90, 90*
  fillets of sole with

herbal beurre blanc, 134
grilled, brochettes, 138
grilled, salad, 138
grouper with Champagne
  saffron cream, 140
lobster ravioli with
  tomato cream sauce,
  124, 125
marinated grilled
  swordfish steaks, 56, 57
sea bass with orange-
  ginger sauce, 139
seared tuna with
  coconut curry sauce,
  134-35, 135
spaghetti with clam
  sauce, 129
Vineyard lobster dip,
  25, 25
see also Crab(s);
  Salmon; Shrimp
Seating arrangements,
  64, 65
Sesame peanut dressing,
  spicy, 115
Shrimp:
  Chardonnay soup, 38
  grilled, with mango
    glacé and plantains,
    132, 133
  grilled seafood
    brochettes, 138
  and plantains on
    skewers with mango
    mayonnaise, 21, 21
Side dishes:
  banana hash, 93, 93
  black-eyed peas with
    smoked turkey, 86
  bourbon corn pudding, 155
  cinnamon fried apples, 157
  garlic mashed potatoes, 74

herb-marinated grilled
  vegetables, 58, 59
jalapeño cornbread,
  88, 89
mango or papaya chutney,
  153, 157
paprika roasted
  potatoes, 156
pigeon peas and rice,
  154, 155
potatoes au gratin, 38
sautéed green peppers
  and tomatoes, 156
tomato salsa, 156-57
see also Salads,
  first-course or side-dish
Smothered pork chops, 148
Sole, fillets of, with
  herbal beurre blanc, 134
Soups:
  berry berry, 106
  black bean, with
    andouille sausage and
    sour cream, 107
  black-eyed pea, with
    smoked turkey, 86, 87
  chicken, Henry's, 105
  chilled mixed melon,
    104, 105
  roasted plum tomato,
    with chèvre croutons,
    36, 37
  shrimp Chardonnay, 38
  sweet corn and crab
    chowder, 108, 109
  tangy gazpacho, 56
  vegetable, Mom's, 106
Spaghetti with clam
  sauce, 129
Spinach fettuccine with
  chicken in spicy
  tomato sauce, 128

Spreads:
  quick black olive, 119
  see also Dips
Strawberries dipped in
  chocolate, 33
Sweet potato pie with
  praline pecan sauce,
  94, 95
Swordfish steaks,
  marinated grilled, 56, 57

TABLES:
  for buffets, 83
  dressing of, 32, 67, 68
  shape of, 65
Tapenade, olive, 119
Tart, herbed onion, 100
Tartar sauce, 90
Theme parties, 47
Tomato(es):
  roasted plum, sauce,
    linguine with, 40, 41
  roasted plum, soup with
    chèvre croutons, 36, 37
  sautéed green peppers
    and, 156
  watercress, and endive
    salad, 39
Tortes:
  flourless chocolate
    nut, 164-65
  mocha, with crème
    anglaise and
    raspberry coulis, 42, 43
Tribeca cocktail, 18
Tricolor pasta salad, 127, 127
Tuiles, coconut, with
  raspberry coulis, 164
Tuna:
  grilled seafood
    brochettes, 138
  seared, with coconut

curry sauce, 134-35, 135
Turkey, smoked, black-
  eyed pea soup with, 86, 87

VALENTINE's dinner for
  kids, 33
Valentine's dinner for
  two, 28-43
  dressing for, 32
  menu for, 32-33, 34
  recipes for, 35-43
  setting and ambience
    for, 30-32
Veal:
  chops with sage, 148, 149
  ground, rigatoni with
    sage and, 129
Vegetable(s):
  curried, in puff
    pastry, 70, 71
  herb-marinated grilled,
    58, 59
  pasta primavera, 126
  soup, Mom's, 106
  see also specific vegetables
Vinaigrettes:
  balsamic, 74
  basil, 115
  citrus, 137
  honey mustard, 119
  lime, 138
  raspberry, 39
Vineyard lobster dip, 25, 25
Volcanic scones, 166

WATERCRESS, tomato, and
  endive salad, 39
Whiting, cornmeal
  pan-fried, 90, 90
Whole wheat potato rolls, 169

YEAST rolls, B. Smith's, 168

DESIGNED BY HELENE SILVERMAN
THE MAIN TYPEFACE IN THIS BOOK IS SCALA,
DESIGNED BY MARTIN MAJOOR
PRINTED AND BOUND BY
TOPPAN PRINTING COMPANY, LTD.
TOKYO, JAPAN